D0056016

TRUST YOUR VIBES AT WORK,

and Let Them Work for *You*

Also by Sonia Choquette

*Ask Your Guides Oracle Cards**

*Diary of a Psychic**

The Psychic Pathway

The Psychic Pathway to Joy

The Psychic Pathway to New Beginnings

*Soul Lessons and Soul Purpose Oracle Cards**

True Balance

*Trust Your Vibes**

*Trust Your Vibes Oracle Cards**

*Vitamins for the Soul**

The Wise Child

Your Heart's Desire

---

*Published by Hay House

Please visit Hay House USA: **www.hayhouse.com**
Hay House Australia: **www.hayhouse.com.au**
Hay House UK: **www.hayhouse.co.uk**
Hay House South Africa: **orders@psdprom.co.za**

TRUST YOUR VIBES AT WORK,

and Let Them Work for *You*

Sonia Choquette

Hay House, Inc.
Carlsbad, California
London • Sydney • Johannesburg
Vancouver • Hong Kong

Published and distributed in the United States by: Hay House, Inc., P.O. Box 5100, Carlsbad, CA 92018-5100 • *Phone:* (760) 431-7695 or (800) 654-5126 • *Fax:* (760) 431-6948 or (800) 650-5115 • www.hayhouse.com • ***Published and distributed in Australia by:*** Hay House Australia Pty. Ltd., 18/36 Ralph St., Alexandria NSW 2015 • *Phone:* 612-9669-4299 • *Fax:* 612-9669-4144 • www.hayhouse.com.au • ***Published and distributed in the United Kingdom by:*** Hay House UK, Ltd. • Unit 62, Canalot Studios • 222 Kensal Rd., London W10 5BN • *Phone:* 44-20-8962-1230 • *Fax:* 44-20-8962-1239 • www.hayhouse.co.uk • ***Published and distributed in the Republic of South Africa by:*** Hay House SA (Pty), Ltd., P.O. Box 990, Witkoppen 2068 • *Phone/Fax:* 27-11-706-6612 • orders@psdprom.co.za • ***Distributed in Canada by:*** Raincoast • 9050 Shaughnessy St., Vancouver, B.C. V6P 6E5 • *Phone:* (604) 323-7100 • *Fax:* (604) 323-2600

Editorial supervision: Jill Kramer • *Design:* Tricia Breidenthal

Hardcover **ISBN 13:** 978-1-4019-0730-3
Hardcover **ISBN 10:** 1-4019-0730-X
Tradepaper **ISBN 13:** 978-1-4019-0731-0
Tradepaper **ISBN 10:** 1-4019-0731-8

Printed in the United States of America

I would like to dedicate this book to my father, whose work ethic sets the standard for mastery, integrity, and love in all he does. To all my professional clients over the past 30 years (you've been my teachers and my inspiration); to my family, who has had the enormous patience to work with me; and to David Smith, for introducing me to Hay House.

CONTENTS

Author's Note: *Every story in this book is true, but most names have been changed to protect the privacy of those concerned.*

fight over limited resources.

Six-sensory people, on the other hand, perceive the world through eyes of possibility and creativity, as an open-ended realm of opportunity with only their imagination limiting their potential. Six-sensories don't engage in the struggle of competition, but operate out of an entirely different paradigm—one that's friendly and receptive to their desires, taking them wherever they want to go, creating whatever they want to create, while bypassing obstacles along the way. Six-sensories never doubt that their personal gifts and talents are being highly received and rewarded.

You may think that this is all very well and good for those who have a sixth sense, but what if you're not one of the lucky ones? Well, the good news is that everyone has a sixth sense—yours may just be lying dormant. Better news is that it can be readily activated and put to use in your work world immediately. And the best news is that this book will teach you how to do just that.

Trusting my vibes and teaching others how to trust theirs, both in work and in life, has been my vocation for more than 35 years. In *Trust Your Vibes at Work, and Let Them Work for You,* I share the best, most effective strategies I know for activating your sixth sense on the job. I acquired them through my own experience and years of studying others. But don't let their simplicity fool you—their very simplicity guarantees success.

If you're ready to stop struggling with fear and doubt about your job and want to flow joyfully with the creative and unlimited forces of the universe; use all your natural resources; reclaim your power as a six-sensory, intuitively guided, creative soul; and truly succeed—then open your mind and let's begin.

That was 20 years ago and a different millennium. Attitudes are changing, and those who are succeeding in today's fickle and furiously competitive work environments are no longer secretive about using their sixth sense as their lodestar for work. They're far too busy reaping their rewards to get hung up on what anyone else thinks.

By leading with their *vibes* (as I call the sixth sense, because it operates as a subtle, vibrating force that centers in the heart and resonates throughout the body), these people are becoming leaders and role models for others. Their vibes not only ensure their personal success, but in many cases also create a positive, successful work environment, providing prosperous jobs and a happy work experience for many others.

I call these intuitive, creative people "six-sensories," because they recognize and actively use their sixth sense as natural and necessary means for achieving success. They don't consider it sixth in importance, but first when making decisions.

Are You a Five- or Six-Sensory Person?

I call people who tune out the sixth sense or allow it to lie dormant "five-sensories" because they rely only on their five physical senses and not their heart-centered, spiritual sixth sense to direct their lives. Five-sensory (or not-yet-six-sensory) people perceive the world through eyes of limitation and fear and are all too easily victimized by what appears to be out of their control—whether it be the economy, bad luck, unscrupulous bosses, unfit or low-paying jobs, or any other problem of the moment. Five-sensories look strictly at superficial appearances and tend to view work as a dog-eat-dog arena where people must

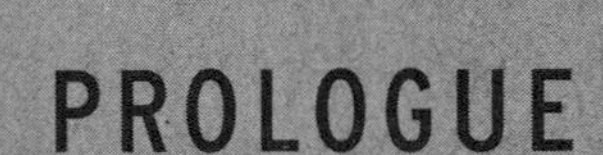

PROLOGUE

My day began at 8:30 A.M., 15 minutes after sending my daughters off to school. I entered my office, opened the blinds, lit my rose-scented candle, greeted my higher forces and spirit helpers, and got ready for my first client.

His name was Stan, a real-estate developer from Houston who owned several properties in limited partnership and a small hotel, all of which were in Texas. He had more than 30 employees, most of whom ran the hotel. After an incredible financial run of good fortune for most of his working life, at age 53 Stan was suddenly faced with myriad problems, and he feared going bankrupt. His hotel was deeply in debt, and a major development in Dallas had failed to attract the investors he needed to move forward.

After going through a very acrimonious divorce and separating from several long-time business partners, Stan was financially depleted, emotionally exhausted, and out of ideas for how to get his momentum back, which is why he came to see me.

Consulting my sixth sense, I could easily see

that Stan had lost the heart and soul for his business, and what used to thrill him at work now felt like the proverbial albatross around his neck. Despite his hope to get reenergized and regain the enthusiasm for his projects that he needed to attract investors, we both knew that it wasn't going to happen because his heart just wasn't in it.

On a creative and soul level, Stan was finished with this phase of his life and was ready for a major professional change, although he couldn't accept it. He also needed a new direction in order to salvage what business he had left—that is, if he didn't want to go broke. The direction in which he'd been headed wasn't working anymore.

My vibes told me that Stan's greatest business mistake through the years had been not empowering those around him, and it was catching up to him. His overly controlling and negative leadership style diminished, rather than developed, his employees—and bit by bit, they'd lost their affection and enthusiasm for him and their jobs. The domino effect led to poor-quality service at the hotel, a lack of employee loyalty, and ultimately, the loss of visitors and income.

Stan had originally attracted wonderful financial people as partners, but he treated them more like employees. They saw his negativity, fear, and overbearing control as major turn-offs; consequently, they walked out, leaving him stranded and alone.

The only thing that could save Stan's business was for him to listen to his heart, get honest fast, let go of control, and admit his desire to move on . . . and then take the steps to do so. He couldn't have freedom and wield absolute control at the same time. He had to choose.

I suggested that Stan turn the hotel over to his brother, Jim, who worked there and loved it. If Stan gave Jim the freedom to run the business as he saw fit and took the risk to fully empower him, Jim's enthusiasm and devotion could, with a lot of work, save the hotel. Stan had never thought of this, yet he agreed that it was a great idea.

The second suggestion was to contact his prior investors and offer them the opportunity to take over his development completely, sell out his interest to them, and be retained solely as a consultant. This would give him the freedom he desired, engage him creatively, and take the burden of management off his back. It would also open the way to a new line of work as a consultant, whereby Stan could sell his fabulous ideas while letting others do the hard work—which he'd briefly entertained but never followed up on.

Finally, I suggested that he take three months off and travel with the new love of his life, something he'd never done but had dreamed of ever since he began working as a teenager. I assured him that he'd come back a new, less burdened, and financially solvent man. The bottom line, I said, was that if he kept the status quo, his business would crash and burn. Sure, he'd be free, but he'd also be broke and probably miserable. The choice was his.

Looking him straight in the eye, I said, "Stan, trust your own vibes for once. You know what to do. It's just a matter of having the courage and willingness to change."

When I was finished, he sat in silence. I asked him if he intuitively resonated with anything I'd suggested. After a long pause, he took a deep breath and quietly admitted that his own vibes agreed with everything I told him. Suddenly he relaxed, and looking me straight in the eye, blurted out, "I get it! It's time for a change. If I don't do this, I'll lose it all—or get sick trying to keep things going as they are."

He drew himself up, and with a decisive shake of the

head, said, "I'm going to do it! It's going to work out, and I know how to do it!" With that, the energy in the room dramatically shifted: Doom and gloom gave way to optimism, and Stan smiled broadly. Yes, he faced an uphill climb, but it was better than falling off a cliff.

If Stan reconnected to his heart, trusted his vibes, and moved in the direction of his true desire, I knew he'd be all right. We said good-bye, and I moved on to my next client.

Seven months later I received a postcard from Tuscany, which said:

Dear Sonia,

I took your advice and trusted my vibes. I'm now a free and solvent man, loving my life, and finally feeling successful. Let me know if you ever need a business consultant, as that is now what I do.

Many thanks,
Stan

P.S. It's beautiful here.

INTRODUCTION

As a professional, six-sensory, intuitive consultant and teacher, I've worked with thousands of people from all over the world who seek my advice and direction, especially regarding their jobs. In fact, job difficulties and dissatisfaction are the main reasons people seek my assistance. Beyond love, relationship, and even health issues, work troubles seem to cause more angst and trauma than all other areas of personal activity combined.

I talk with people daily—young and old, highly educated and self-made, entrepreneurial and artsy, blue- and white-collar, and everything in between—and the problems they struggle with regarding work are universal. Every day I hear variations on the same theme: "I don't like my work"; "I don't like the people I work with"; "I feel uninspired"; "I feel unappreciated and unimportant on the job"; "I want to work for myself, but I'm afraid I'll fail"; "I fear I'll lose my job, fail to advance in my job, or have a takeover eliminate my job"; "I'm bored with my job and feel like I'm wasting time there"; and last, but hardly least, "I don't make enough money on the job, or at the minimum, the money I think I'm worth."

For many of my clients and students, work woes have become all-consuming, and in these uncertain economic times, such concerns seem to have completely taken over their lives, filling them with anxiety and stress. Yet I have a special group who are in every sense of the word masters of the game in the arena of work, who are immune to employment issues of any kind. They love their jobs, prosper year after year in both good economic climates and bad, and can hardly wait to get to work each day. They spend quality time with their families, take frequent vacations, and even retire early (although some can but don't because they're having too much fun to stop).

Are these trust-fund babies? Harvard graduates? Lottery winners? Or are they just plain lucky? None of the above—they're ordinary folks like you and me. Many are self-made, some are only minimally educated, and more than a few are "nonprofessional," yet they all have one crucial quality in common, which virtually guarantees them 100 percent satisfaction and success in their work. The secret ingredient isn't an MBA, exceptional talent or skill, or unbelievable luck. It's this: *These people have made the simple decision to always, and in all ways, listen to and trust their sixth sense to guide them in their working life.*

In the early '80s, *Harvard Business Review* conducted a survey of the top 100 American CEOs in which they were asked to name the one factor, above all others, that contributed to their phenomenal success. The surprising (though not to me) answer by all 100 was that they listened to their gut instinct or intuition. What I thought was amusing was the unanimous corollary that they didn't like to advertise the fact that it was their sixth sense that took them to the top—they were fearful that their peers wouldn't approve.

GETTING READY

In this book I'll introduce you to 29 six-sensory strategies (one at a time) for activating, sharpening, and mastering your vibes at work:

— In **Part I**, the first nine tactics focus on training your body and basic awareness to become sensitive to your sixth sense on the job, especially under pressure. They center on creating a solid foundation upon which to access your vibes as you need them.

— The next 11 strategies in **Part II** build upon those first 9, but they also provide a platform to organize your intuitive awareness and allow it to comfortably operate at an even higher level of sophistication and creativity than ever before.

— **Part III** is intended to take your intuitive skills to a mastery level, allowing them to become second nature and take you to the top of your professional game. If you use the suggestions here, you're guaranteed to have a prosperous, creative, and satisfying professional life.

Each strategy builds on the one before, allowing you a gradual and easy ascent into becoming a six-sensory professional. Some may be familiar—maybe you even already use them—while others might seem new, exotic, and even risky. Be open-minded, and practice each tactic at your own pace, setting your own course of action. Then note what happens. In that way you'll learn to trust your vibes based on your own experiences. If you give each strategy a fair chance, I assure you that you'll see immediate, direct, and positive results.

Do Your Homework

In order to track your vibes to see how well they serve you, you'll need a small pocket notebook so that you can jot things down as you work with this book. The benefit of keeping track of what occurs is that you won't have to trust *me* that this works. Rather, you'll be able to see for yourself how trustworthy your vibes are on the job . . . once you get them working for you.

The other bit of homework I'm going to assign is visualization exercises. Doing them for a few minutes in the morning before you start your day will activate your intuitive muscles. View these exercises as business meetings with your higher consciousness, where *you* are the CEO.

By using these two tools every day, you'll soon be on your way to leading a charmed, exciting, and prosperous business life. The greatest challenge will be adjusting to a life that runs smoothly; finances that flow easily; and a day-to-day existence that's exciting, but free of extreme stress or drama. If that appeals to you, then let's get on with it!

PART I

Basic Training

STRATEGY #1

SET YOUR INTENTION

If you truly want to be a six-sensory leader in your world, you must set the intention to do so. It's important that you begin each workday with a clear idea of what you hope to achieve, especially if you want to be intuitively guided toward reaching your greatest potential.

I remind clients all the time that intuition doesn't drop from nowhere, as some people would like to believe. Instead, it directly follows your natural interests and intentions, and supports what's most important to you. So if you come to work with no set intentions, you won't be divinely inspired because your creative doors will be shut.

However, if you come in with clearly defined goals, everything in your conscious, subconscious, and higher mind will focus on supporting them. One of my favorite quotes is from the *I Ching,* "The Chinese Book of Changes": "The way it begins is the way it ends." In other words, your relationship to your job can only be set by you. You may choose to only do what you're told and nothing more, but you'll find little creativity or inspiration in that.

It's far more exciting and rewarding to see your job as your personal kingdom where you determine your own goals and challenges. For example, you might follow a hunch to reorganize your showroom to better feature a new product, or you may act on an impulse to take a long-term client out to lunch in appreciation of her loyalty. Mentally visit your kingdom every morning, checking all aspects of it, and then set the day's course according to what you observed there and what you intend to create.

The best way to determine your intentions is to develop the art of visualization. Get up 15 minutes earlier than usual, and while still in bed, review everything you scheduled for that day. Decide what you hope to create and achieve from each task. At the same time, honestly assess your emotional and mental approach to each event: Are you looking forward to it, or are you hesitant and resistant? If you're feeling negative, what's causing your discomfort? The more specifically you can preview your day, the more clarity and receptivity you'll invite in from your intuitive mind during work. Ask yourself these basic questions: "What do I have scheduled today?" "What do I want to get out of this experience?" and "How do I feel about the events I have in place?" Then pay attention to your responses.

If you're uncomfortable about anything, ask yourself what the exact nature of your insecurity is. What's the worst thing that can happen, for instance, when you must cold-call a customer or undertake a project that feels intimidating? Then ask what the best possible outcome is that you can hope to achieve in the same situation so that your Higher Self can aspire to it. Find out what your greatest weakness is, as well as what could block your goals or interfere with your intentions. Then decide on the areas where you could use your intuition.

After your preview, set your course for the day, remaining clear on your goals and being open to higher inspiration. Using your imagination, create a place in your mind for your inner genius to speak directly to you while at work. Even go so far as to give your intuition a name and speak directly to it when you need guidance or direction. I call my intuitive genius "Bright Idea," and I talk to it many times during the day, on every issue that challenges me. I simply say, "Bright Idea, what would you do in this situation?" And then I listen.

The more defined your work goals are, the more your intuition can help. For example, my client Cecelia was recruited to head a new division at a large pharmaceutical company in Ohio. She was asked to turn the entire division around from a costly slump and restore it to productivity, and she knew that she was inheriting a hostile and ineffective staff. Terrified, but challenged, she took the job.

When we spoke, I counseled Cecelia to set her intentions and vigorously go after them. She took my advice and systematically began envisioning each day before going to work. In doing so, she realized that there was no sense of team spirit, as most employees were in survival, rather than creative, mode. In other words, it was "every man for himself."

Cecelia began each day by mentally recruiting various employees to her winning team, gaining their confidence and enthusiasm, one at a time, for making their division the best in the Midwest. To her surprise, her efforts made a difference: Many lethargic workers were won over; those who weren't, quit.

Asking herself what she avoided, it was clearly the oldest manager. He was hostile, ineffective, defensive, agitating to others, and chronically late. Cecelia's logic said to fire or transfer him, and she intended to do just that. During their meeting, however, her intuition led her down another road, telling her to give him a new assignment and title and recruit him to her cause.

Going against conventional wisdom because her vibes were so strong, she took a risk. Rather than giving him his walking papers, which he fully expected, Cecelia asked the man if he'd be interested in a promotion and taking on the assignment of building team morale.

Stunned, he replied, "Me? Are you serious?"

"Yes," she said. "You know best what's wrong here, so who better to fix it? You can turn your dissatisfaction into useful insight to improve things, or you can leave. In either case, something must improve, and now. What's your choice?"

Thus, an unusual alliance was born. The team was built, and the division turned around in three months. Cecelia's intuition and daily visioning to set her intention paid off. And she couldn't have picked a better quarterback, because her division has been the company leader for the past three years. Last I heard, Cecelia was being recruited to help another failing division on the West Coast, a place she'd always wanted to live. I wonder if she accepted.

5 TIPS FOR SETTING INTENTIONS

1. Wake up 15 minutes earlier.
2. Before rising, mentally review your schedule for the day ahead.
3. Imagine each person or situation that you'll face, along with the outcome you want to create with each one.
4. Visualize every encounter, project, and assignment flowing smoothly.
5. Breathing deeply as you see your day, leave room for even greater successes than you can imagine—and expect the best!

Do not underestimate the power of envisioning your day. A few minutes spent imagining wonderful things on the job in the morning can turn an ordinary day into a miracle-making one. Last week, for example, I woke up and had the sudden inspiration to be featured on national television in some way. I allowed myself the fun of seeing it happen without concerning myself with *how* it would happen. I simply imagined it, and then went to work in my home office.

When I finished consulting with my clients that afternoon, my assistant told me that another author I was scheduled to go on tour with later this year had mentioned me in an interview she was giving on national television. So there it was: As I worked in my office, my visualization turned into reality. My teachers always taught me that you can't create what you can't imagine, yet you always create what you *do* imagine. So start your day by exercising your envisioning muscles, and enjoy the outcome.

Your Turn

Before even getting out of bed in the morning, call to mind the events you're going to face during the day. One by one, focus your attention on each event and envision how you want it to go. What do you hope to accomplish? What do you see as the best possible outcome? What would you like to create? As you envision, pay attention to any resistance to your success. What obstacles are in the way? What, if anything, should you avoid?

Envision the best possible solutions and set your intentions to create them by speaking them out loud. Then take the time to reinforce your intentions by jotting them down in your pocket notebook. Also, come up with a name for your inner genius and ask it to go to work with you. Leave the door open for your intuition to lead, and listen carefully throughout the day

THE BOTTOM LINE:

Positively visualize your day before it begins.

STRATEGY #2

GET GROUNDED

The best way to sail through your business day guided by higher awareness and intuitive, creative flow is to begin in an energetically grounded, calm state and practice remaining that way no matter what happens.

Being grounded means that you don't allow your psychic circuits to overload and shut down. It means remaining centered in your body, committed to your goals, unafraid of others' opinions, and capable of making solid decisions that support your overall well-being.

In today's sensory-overloaded business world, being grounded is easier said than done. With information downloading into our brains at record levels, it's no wonder that so many people find themselves short-circuiting. Being bombarded by countless means of communication stresses our nervous systems, agitates our emotions, and jumbles our thoughts if we don't do something to manage the input.

You know you're ungrounded when your heart races, your anxiety level rises, your breathing becomes more shallow, your temper starts to flare, and you feel stressed and in a state of emergency, like the Cat in the Hat juggling too many plates in the air at once. And when you're not grounded at work, it feels as though there's no room for error, leaving you threatened and afraid. Other signs are not listening, being unable to concentrate, and failing to follow through on what you're doing.

When I consult with clients, I'm astounded at how many work issues and struggles boil down to nothing more than a bunch of ungrounded people setting each other off in a psychic frenzy. Now there are lots of reasons we become ungrounded at work, and very few have anything to do with the job itself:

— The first is **not getting enough sleep.** Your body processes a lot of information in a day, and if it's exhausted, it simply cannot absorb all the input.

— **Hunger or overstimulation** by too much caffeine and sugar may also contribute to your feeling "at loose ends." If you start your day with coffee and a doughnut before you get to work, you're doomed before you even begin.

Not only does having an overall healthy diet play an important role in strengthening your ability to pay attention (a basic key to intuitive awareness), but eating enough protein in the morning is also a key to being grounded. Your brain requires this nutrient to process information; inadequate amounts are tremendously stressful and ungrounding. A simple protein bar or drink stashed in your desk may be all you need.

— **Dehydration** is a third offender. Drinking water regularly during the day keeps you hydrated and your blood flowing and open creatively.

— **Sitting too long** is extremely ungrounding. Standing up, stretching, or even walking across the office helps download any excess energy and allows you to process and absorb it more effectively.

Fortunately, getting grounded is easy . . . if you remember to do it. The quickest way to shift out of your brain and reconnect to your body is through exercise and movement. If you feel overloaded, you can immediately stop the inflow by standing up and moving around. Go to the watercooler, the bathroom, even outside if possible—don't just sit in psychic meltdown.

The best way to remain grounded day in and day out is to start exercising: 10 to 15 minutes on a treadmill, StairMaster, or elliptical trainer clears the psychic fog and restores clarity. (If you don't have that much time, three to five minutes of moving will ground you immediately. Breathing is another good technique: Inhale through your nose and exhale through your mouth until your heartbeat is regular and calm.)

Many of my professional clients have taken up jogging as a way to get grounded, especially those who travel a great deal. Jake, a high-powered international banker, gave up room service and two glasses of wine and instead took up running after he arrived at a new business destination.

"Between jet lag, time changes, language barriers, strange places, and unfamiliar people, I realized that I was extremely ungrounded most of the time I was working," he said. "I ignored my state of being, or numbed it with too much food, too many drinks, and too much television. Realizing that the low-grade anxiety I felt was simply being ungrounded, I changed my habits and addressed the problem.

"I took my running shoes with me wherever I went, and as soon as possible after landing, I'd go for a short jog—followed by a long shower, a bottle of water, and a good dinner. The results were amazing: I showed up at work far more centered and better able to do business."

The grounded person in the office is easily identified, and the most valuable to the team. He or she is the one you go to in order to get things done without drama, the one you can count on to be efficient and direct without wasting time with excuses. Two or three minutes spent with a grounded individual calms your anxiety at work and keeps everyone on track.

My assistant, Ryan, is one such person. At times my office can feel very much like a hospital ER, as we field an endless stream of crises from clients who feel that they need immediate attention, even if I'm out. Cool, calm, and collected, Ryan sips his water, stretches his legs, takes a deep breath, and tells my clients not to worry—everything will work out. He does the same for me: His grounded vibration slows everything to a manageable pace, separating emotion from reason, drama from reality, and problem from solution. His contribution is so enormous that I elevated his position twice in the first year, and I even turned the management of my entire consulting practice over to him.

So not only is becoming grounded an important and essential tool in business, it can be the very skill that will take you to the top. No matter what business you're in, being well grounded assures a positive outcome. The *I Ching* emphasizes the importance and power of this state, especially for leaders, when it says: "The general drinks from the well first; then, and only then, can he truly lead the army."

Everyone wants the grounded person to remain on board because he or she calms the atmosphere and gets things done without incident. It's insurance that will always take you to the top of your business ladder.

8 TIPS FOR STAYING GROUNDED THROUGHOUT THE DAY

1. Use a good pillow so that you can sleep better.
2. Get a water-filtration system at home and ask for one at work.
3. Eat a good breakfast, skipping sugar and that second cup of coffee. Have a protein bar or an egg instead.
4. On your break, walk around the block.
5. If your company offers a membership to a gym, take it. If not, consider parking a few blocks away and walking the rest of the way to the office.
6. Skip the cigarettes and breathe slowly, deeply, and often.
7. Turn off your radio, stereo, cell phone, and iPod and enjoy the peace and quiet of an "unstimulated" moment on the way to and from work.
8. Recognize the importance and value of being a grounded professional.

Your Turn

This week, practice getting and staying grounded. Start each day by giving yourself more time to get ready for work so that you can eat a good breakfast and get there at a comfortable pace. If possible, walk the last few blocks to the office—take your time and enjoy the experience. Throughout the day, get up and move around often. Drink water instead of coffee, and go to the gym or take in a little exercise before going home. If necessary, treat yourself to a great new pillow and go to bed a little earlier.

Make notes in your pocket notebook on events and situations that caused you to become ungrounded during the day, and plan for ways to keep this from happening in the future. For example, "I didn't allow time for road construction this morning, so I became ungrounded as I raced to work on an alternate route. I need to leave 15 minutes earlier tomorrow." "I realized today that I get hypoglycemic and need to eat a snack around 10:30 in order to think clearly. Remind myself to bring one tomorrow." Or "My assistant was disorganized at the meeting and this ungrounded me. I need to check in with him before meetings to make sure that we're prepared."

If you jot down these notes for a week, you'll begin to see a pattern of what "ungrounds" you on a regular basis. Then, with this information right in front of you, you can plan ways to prevent this from happening in the future and stay in your power.

THE BOTTOM LINE:

Stay grounded.

STRATEGY #3

BECOME ORGANIZED

The most concrete obstacle to accessing your intuition at work is being disorganized. Intuition is the ability to perceive subtle direction coming from a higher vibration, and to have such acute perception, you must have keen awareness. If you swim in a sea of constant disarray with a backlog of unfinished business, or you're buried under a mountain of sloppy paper, chances are high that you'll fail to perceive even the most obvious circumstances around you, let alone intercept the more subtle, intuitive insights that should guide your work decisions.

If you're not organized, you won't be able to tap in to your vibes. Your sixth sense relays a constant flow of information from your subconscious, telepathic intuition to your conscious awareness—but in order to dial in to and make use of it, you must have a calm, receptive, and organized mind. The best way to do so is to establish your priorities and plan around them.

Your priorities can be found by identifying those goals that you really care about right now. Your intuition can then fully align with your focus, giving you constant guidance for fulfilling your goals. If your goals aren't focused, life gets crazy, inviting anxiety and confusion, overwhelming any intuitive communication coming your way.

Start by making a list of the ten most important goals you have *right now.* Forget ultimate goals, as they're too vague and impractical. For example, if you eventually want to start your own business, but at the moment you're going to graduate school, are in the middle of a divorce, or are in the process of moving, set aside your future dreams and focus on the practical needs of graduating, getting divorced, or finding a new home. I've found that the more immediate and specific your intentions, the more effectively your intuition will work.

Once you identify your short-term goals, take a critical look at how you spend your time: Do you generally spend it moving toward your goals or away from them? Begin to immediately eliminate the things that distract you. If you can't, then recognize their importance to your goals and adjust accordingly. For example, if your goal is to call at least three new prospective clients a day yet you never get to it because you spend all morning catching up on phone calls, then make "returning phone calls" one of your goals. If your goal is to finish your project by the end of the week, but you spend two days in meetings to get approval on your changes, then add "scheduling essential meetings" to your goals.

Next, look around at your desk, office, and work environment: Is there anything that's cluttered, overflowing, or doesn't serve your needs? A disorganized mess disturbs and scrambles your intuitive channels, causing you to miss out on important insights and opportunities. As you clear your surroundings, you'll clear your higher channels as well.

A contractor friend of mine had been procrastinating about cleaning his office for years. He'd accumulated a mound of old blueprints, job orders, finished project contracts, and piles of samples from every building supplier in the business. He could barely find his way from the front door to his desk, leaving him greatly behind schedule most of the time.

One day, feeling extremely hassled by missed deadlines, he decided to get rid of the mess. Ignoring all the bad advice he'd received over the years to hold on to things because he might need them someday, he ruthlessly threw everything out but his desk, phone, computer, and fax. By the time he was done, he felt as though he'd climbed out from under a mountain of mess.

Sitting at his freshly emancipated desk, he began his day anew. And when the phone rang, he was able to give his mostly irate clients his full attention. Freed from the need to sort through stuff to defend his lateness, he simply listened to their complaints. He resolved most issues then and there, using both common sense and an unexpected surge of intuition. In three months he went from being the "hated builder" to being invited to dinner by his clients. Maintaining his clear-desk policy, he grew his business by 20 percent in less than a year.

As you can see, disorganization is a costly energy leak both for your intuition and your business. Look at your surroundings and see if they reflect order, balance, and organization—after all, intuition and creativity require attention and calm energy.

THE NEXT AREA THAT NEEDS ORGANIZATION is your time. I observe, especially with my more ambitious clients, that they allow themselves to become way too overscheduled, which causes them to frantically rush through the day to catch up. It may feel exciting, and they may even be able to do it, but I can assure you that working in such a frantic mode doesn't allow room for creativity and inspiration.

Please keep this in mind: *You need time to tap in to your intuition.* I realize that for many people, work is relentless and the pace can't be controlled. But you *can* control what takes your attention.

5 WAYS TO ORGANIZE AND SAVE YOUR TIME

1. Screen your phone calls (or keep them short).
2. Cut back on Web surfing.
3. Check your e-mail only on your break.
4. The same goes for chatting with others.
5. Prioritize your next day's work before you leave the office every evening.

Now I'm not trying to suggest that you become overly mechanical and linear; just be selective about what takes your time. Even more important is the need to schedule daily quiet time. You don't need to take a nap (but if you can, do!), just grab a few minutes here and there to allow your brain to rest and your vibes to speak. When you schedule appointments, for example, give yourself an extra five minutes between clients to sit quietly. Taking these breaks isn't wasting time—rather, they allow your inner perceptions to rise to the surface. They could very well be the most important and efficient minutes you spend in a day.

Finally, if you can't slow your pace, at least slow your breathing. Rushing around tends to put you in a state of "fight or flight," causing you to breathe shallowly or even hold your breath, thus disconnecting yourself completely from your higher awareness. When you find yourself in "race mode," focus on your breathing: Inhale deeply and slowly through your nose and then exhale through your mouth, gently saying "Aah" as you do. And move your neck and shoulders to release tension. Practice this for just a minute or two—that's enough to reconnect to your creative and intuitive channels.

Your Turn

This week, clear your office or work space of any unnecessary clutter. Be brutal in eliminating any- and everything that doesn't support your current professional goals. If you have unfinished business, finish it. If you're overbooked, contact your appointments and reschedule. It's better for a client or employee to have your full attention than to spend time with you when you aren't really there because you're playing catch-up.

A clear desk creates a clear mind, which is the best kind for intuitive reception. Guard your timetable and be highly selective about how you commit yourself. Allow more time between appointments or projects to tune in to your higher awareness. Slow down and breathe slowly as you find a proper pace.

Using your pocket notebook, write down your ten most important goals for the week, along with the time you intend to use to accomplish them. Check them off as you succeed in meeting these goals. Also, note anything that wastes your time so that you're aware of it when making commitments in the future.

THE BOTTOM LINE:

Clear the decks.

STRATEGY #4

STIMULATE YOUR CREATIVITY

One of the most frequent complaints I hear from leaders in the business world is the lack of creativity, self-direction, and innovation displayed by their employees. The flip side of this coin is the nonstop complaining from employees who say that their jobs are boring and their workplaces dreary and depressing. The minute I hear these complaints on either side, I know that the problem is a failure of the work to capture the employees' imagination.

Over and over again I hear bosses lament the lack of enthusiasm and problem-solving on the part of their employees, yet these same employers put their workers in severe cubicles, and worse, surround them with dreary wall colors, harsh fluorescent lighting, and the ambiance of a funeral parlor.

If we're going to be intuitively productive, then we need to feed our senses better than this—after all, creativity *is* born from the senses. Most people in the business world are sensory deprived, operating under "creative house arrest." In other words, they're regimented to the point that all spontaneity is checked at the door, leaving them to suffer what I call "psychic anorexia," or basic starvation of the inner self, the creative, intuitive part.

Most of the time creativity isn't even welcome on the job, so given the overly serious and rigid atmosphere they toil in, people don't dare share an original idea even if they *are* inspired. The great irony is that more and more businesses I consult with are experiencing a huge exodus of creative talent, and they're screaming at me to stop the creative hemorrhage. Well, Mr. or Ms. Employer, if you want the talent to stay, thrive, and contribute, you as a leader must establish an attitude and an atmosphere on the job that freely invites intuitive and creative brainstorming.

To bring out your (or your employees') best, it helps to create an atmosphere that inspires your inner genius to express itself naturally. That means you need to ease up on the rigidity and introduce humor, playfulness, and an uninhibited and uncensored sharing of ideas. The best way to do so is to stimulate your other five senses with sound, smell, color, flavor, and touch.

Intuitive people tend to be sensual, spontaneous individuals who don't get "stuck in their heads." Creating a playful atmosphere where you feel relaxed and at ease works best for getting you "out of your head" and into your more spontaneous, creative side and turns the intuitive switch on immediately. This doesn't mean that you must turn the office into *Romper Room,* but it does suggest that creating a designated "room to romp" at the office will pay off in increased creativity and inspiration.

7 TIPS FOR INSPIRING CREATIVITY AT WORK

1. Designate a specific room or place on the job to be used as "Creativity and Rejuvenation Central."
2. Add stimulating colors to the walls.
3. Use full-spectrum (instead of fluorescent) lights overhead.
4. Play lively music in the background.
5. Place a placard above the door clearly marking your creative intentions, such as "Creative Laboratory" or "Genius at Work."
6. Designate a "free zone" or free time at work to muse, enthuse, experiment, and brainstorm risk-free.
7. Make available colored markers, chalkboards, crayons, Play-Doh, water pistols, and even musical instruments.

You need to give yourself and your workers things that soothe, seduce, stimulate, and entice your senses. The more you feed your senses, the more sensitive you'll become. The more sensitive to subtle awareness you become, the more your sleeping sixth sense (your intuitive genius within) will wake up. And the more intuitive you are, the more creative you'll be—and you'll tend to make more money. So stimulating creativity is good for business.

The husband of one of my editors does a lot of work for TV and commercial-production houses, and he told me that there are often pinball machines, pool tables, and other "toys" on hand at these offices. I'm not surprised—they have the right idea, and I'm sure it helps their employees do a better job. So, following their example, install anything and everything you need to introduce spontaneity and imagination (the front door to intuition) in *your* office. As the boss, encourage your workers to freely use this space and go there often. And don't worry about them playing too much and neglecting the job—studies have proven over and over that places where people are encouraged to play are 90 percent more self-directed and efficient than places that are "strictly business."

My client Steve was, in my opinion, an absolute creative genius, but he worked for a highly organized yet very serious and humorless software company. Bored out of his mind with this overly regimented and unimaginative environment, he, not surprisingly, became stubborn, unproductive, and slow on the job, acting passive-aggressively most of the time. Of course, he got fired.

When Steve came to me, he was extremely upset and worried about his future. Even though he hated the job, he needed both the money and the reputation of being a responsible person. He was a single father whose ex-wife considered him a screwup, so he thought that what happened proved her right.

Angry and panicked, he was surprised when I congratulated him for getting out of that company, albeit it in a less-than-graceful way. His salary was minimal, the atmosphere was hostile, and worst of all, his endless brilliant resources didn't get tapped—and they never would.

When I asked him how long his unemployment insurance would last, he said six months. I said this was great—for the next two months, he should invite one or two friends over who shared his software interests and do nothing but play computer games all day. He should goof off, hang out, and have fun.

Astounded, Steve told me that he'd go broke and lose

custody of his son. I assured him that he wouldn't, and I asked him to just trust me and try it. He left thinking I was crazy . . . but he took my advice anyway, mostly because everything in him leapt with joy at my suggestion, even though his responsible "work brain" was horrified at the thought.

Three months later he called to say that he'd started his own software company with two other friends, creating computer games. He'd played such games nonstop with his friends and his son all day, as I'd suggested. As a result, Steve and his friends began to brainstorm, and following their intuition, they invented more than 20 new games that were fresh, fun, and quite simply, fantastic. They formed a corporation and took these games to a Japanese software distributor Steve knew from his previous job, and they were so impressed that they signed a million-dollar deal on the spot. He was astonished, but I wasn't. Steve was a wealth of intuitive gold just waiting to be tapped.

THE FIRST REACTION MOST PEOPLE have when I suggest making work more playful is that they'll get in trouble for playing instead of being serious and working. Yet every genius, including Einstein, has conveyed the notion that their only regret was that they didn't allow themselves to play more—because if they had, they would have created more.

When people come to my office, they're often surprised to see that the shelves are filled with dolls, toys, and talismans. I have stuffed animals; musical instruments; and crayons, pencils, paper, and clay.

One client who owned a trucking firm walked in, took one look, and said, "My God, it's *Romper Room* in here!"

"Yes, it is," I replied. "Now, while we're talking, which toy do you want to play with?" He chose the Slinky.

Although I may have an office full of toys and fun things, I'm serious about my play: When I consult with clients, I doodle, draw, toss a ball, look at my dolls, shuffle card decks, or dabble on my flute (which I don't play very well). As I do all this, I get ideas, come up with inventions, and find hundreds of solutions for not only *my* business challenges, but for others' concerns as well. Do my clients mind? Well, I'm presently committed to new clients for the next year and a half, based strictly upon referrals, so apparently not.

If you are aren't the boss, take a chance and ask your employer if he or she would consider creating a space to serve as an intuitive and creative rejuvenation incubator in your place of business. It's easy enough to do, and maybe you might offer to do it yourself (the lunchroom would work fine if there's no other area). Don't assume that you'll be shot down—if you're more productive, your boss will notice and not mind your methods. After all, Leonardo da Vinci, quite possibly the most creative man to ever have lived, once said, "All perceptions arise out of feeding the senses," so you might share this information.

If you can't recruit your employer to the cause, at least create a personal creative space on your desk, in a drawer, or in your briefcase. Start with a few colored markers, some Play-Doh or clay, and a plant or two. And keep in mind that most extremely successful people will tell you that getting to where they got was as much fun as it was work.

Successful businesspeople intuitively know this, like the CEOs of Southwest Airlines and Saturn: Playfulness and humor are job requirements and part of the interview process at these companies. While other industries have suffered immeasurably during the last decade, posting catastrophic losses even before 9/11, these companies sailed through the difficulties by intuitively following a creative, playful work ethic. They literally laughed and played their way to the top.

Your Turn

This week, give your inner genius a happier playground. Ease up on the heavy-handed, puritanical work ethic that's so prevalent today, and have some *fun* on the job. Change your work atmosphere from severe to soft, from black-and-white to color, from heavy to lighthearted. Make your workplace brighter by adding spice, pizzazz, color, and sound to the environment. Add stimulating music—even rock 'n' roll—if you need a boost. Bring games and toys to dabble with. And doodle in your notebook for a few minutes every day.

Do all you can to lighten up on the linear thinking, and let your lighter side out to come out and play at work. You'll be impressed with the results.

THE BOTTOM LINE:

Lighten up and be playful.

STRATEGY #5

CREATE A SACRED WORKPLACE

Six-sensories recognize that their work environment takes on a vibe, a mood, and an energy of its own, so beyond the need to keep it bright and stimulating, they strive to create an ambiance that maintains good vibes in their workplace. They know that the better the vibes, the greater the productivity and success.

Have you ever entered a business and immediately reacted to the vibes, especially negative ones? I know I have. There was once a restaurant on Halsted Street in Chicago that had such notoriously bad vibes that no matter who owned it or how aggressively they redecorated or revamped the place, the funky vibes still remained. In spite of eight or nine efforts to reinvent the place, it always failed. It was dark, dreary, and depressing, and the people who worked there were, too. The restaurant was eventually closed for good; a few years later, it was torn down and a bank was put in its place. The bad vibes won, and only destroying it and starting over worked—such is the power of vibes in the workplace.

Whether you're an employee, are self-employed,

or an employer, step back and objectively assess the energetic tone of your workplace. (Also do this if you're interviewing for a job there.) Ask yourself if it inspires you. Does the energy feel positive, cheerful, uplifting, and pleasant—or is it sterile, dreary, or scary? Studies show that the better the energy and ambiance, the more happy, motivated, and productive the workers will be.

If you're the boss and have a say about the environment, don't be cheap, because it can cost you dollars in the long run. If you're an employee and aren't sure you have a say, ask. And if you're interviewing for a job and don't like what you're feeling, leave.

If you do find the vibes at work a downer, it isn't the end of the road. You can improve the energy right away by taking a few simple steps. Hang up an interesting photo or piece of art to brighten the room, place fresh flowers on your desk, or display things that speak to your heart and bring you good cheer—doing these small things creates big changes in the energy you work in all day. The better the vibe, the better you'll feel and perform.

If you aren't free to create this kind of atmosphere in the open work area, you can still create your own private area of good vibes. Whatever floats your boat, as my teenagers like to say. Name it and bring it—and its positive energy—to work.

10 WAYS TO CREATE A SACRED ATMOSPHERE

1. Add an aquarium.
2. Hang mirrors for better light.
3. Use a fountain.
4. Post positive sayings in the lunchroom.
5. Supply natural springwater.
6. Employ aromatherapy.
7. Keep a clean and bright restroom.
8. Maintain cleanliness in the rest of the office as well.
9. Use soothing ambient light.
10. Have ionizers circulate fresh air.

If you can't make major changes to improve your surroundings, don't worry. Something as simple as taping a cartoon from the newspaper to your computer to make you smile—or placing a sacred talisman that inspires you (such as a small statue of Buddha), a picture of your family, or even a nature scene on your desk can make all the difference in the world when it comes to creating good vibes.

What you choose is up to you, but do pick something. It's important to have a reminder that your work space is sacred. You spend a lot of time there, and it provides income, security, and creative opportunities for you and your family. Respect it, and treat it as the hallowed place it is.

I've personally achieved that. The minute clients walk into my office, regardless of the frame of mind they're in or the crises they're facing, they say, "What great vibes in here." And then they relax.

When we surround ourselves with good vibes, it calms us and opens our hearts and minds so that creativity and higher energy become possible. And besides, positive energy establishes trust between you and your clients as well.

Eileen was just beginning a freelance writing career, so she sought my assistance in helping her get past a major case of writer's block. Try as she might, she'd been unable to compose anything meaningful for months, and money was becoming a serious problem. Not wanting to get a full-time job to pay her bills, she came to me for help.

The first thing I noticed energetically was that her workplace had a very negative and depressing effect on her. When I questioned her about this, she was surprised. She said that she hadn't paid attention to her work space in that way, but now that she thought about it, it could be true. She'd shared her area with another freelance writer for several months because she needed the rent break. Unfortunately, he was extremely negative and constantly demoralized her, telling her that she'd never survive as a writer in this brutal world. Eventually, Eileen couldn't stand it anymore and asked him to leave. Although happy to be alone, she was still unable to write—she didn't consciously recognize it, but I believe it was due to the other writer's lingering "downer" energy.

I suggested that the way to dispel such deadening vibes was to see if anything of the departed tenant remained; if so, she should clear it out. Eileen realized that she'd indeed overlooked some things that he'd left: an ugly lamp without a shade on the far side of room, a gray vase with dreary artificial flowers in the window, and a chipped mirror standing against the wall, all of which depressed her.

She also peered out the window for the first time in months and saw that her view was of an abandoned construction site. *No wonder I'm stuck,* she thought, *considering what I have to inspire me here. This place is dismal and sad.*

Following my suggestion, she immediately set about reclaiming and reviving her space into one she'd love. She removed all of the other writer's leftover junk; then she bought a soft beige floor-to-ceiling window shade to let the light in (but block the view), and a beautiful vase for her desk that she began filling with fresh flowers. She also brought in a lovely large antique lamp with a natural "daylight" bulb to replace the ugly lamp and cold, fluorescent lights overhead. As a final touch of inspiration, she added a small bowl with two blue fish to brighten her mood and keep her company.

Not having enough money to buy expensive art for her bare walls, Eileen took photos of various city sights that she loved and had them blown up and framed. After her redecorating efforts were complete, she laughingly told me that she felt like an artist again and looked forward to going to her office to write. Not surprisingly, her writer's block was cured in no time. The first thing she wrote, in fact, detailed her experience with writer's block and how her office beautification project cured it. The editor of a local magazine liked what Eileen had written and came to her office to see it for herself, and the article was published.

In retrospect, Eileen realized how being cheap and indifferent to her workspace was insulting to her sensitive and creative spirit, causing her to shut down. Once she'd beautified and sanctified her environment, her creative spirit was seduced back into business.

Creating a sacred workspace is so important to your creative and intuitive spirit and so influential to your productivity that whenever you find yourself in a slump at work (or find your employees dragging in their efforts), one of the best things you can do to reenergize the work space is to redecorate.

Greg was a CPA client of mine who suddenly ended a long-term, strained partnership with another accountant. Although he was happy to be free of his partner, Greg's employees were disturbed and confused by the unexpected change; consequently, they became distracted, gossipy, and insecure in their jobs.

Eager to get things back on track as quickly as possible, Greg called in a professional feng shui specialist, whose job was to create an energetically flowing and sacred workplace to ensure success and prosperity. The first thing she did was place a large mirror at the front of the office and add a beautiful fountain in the entry. She rearranged desks, changed the paint colors, added mirrors and fresh flowers, and even moved walls to invigorate the energy and infuse the office with good vibes. She told everyone that she was going to make the office a sacred and safe place to work. They loved hearing that and looked forward to what she was doing.

Apparently her efforts worked: Within 24 hours of the final touches of the face-lift, everyone was bubbling with genuine excitement about the changes, expressing their delight and pride in their newly empowered and beautified space. They were especially vocal about how the energy on the job shifted since she'd arrived, as well as how grateful they were to be blessed with this new sacred space. Not only did Greg's employees forget about the upsetting changes they'd been through, but they threw themselves into their jobs with an enthusiasm he hadn't seen in years.

Interestingly, during this time two people quit, voluntarily eliminating themselves from the commitment to good energy that Greg had set in motion. They were too set in their negative ways to appreciate or join in the office renaissance. They weren't missed.

To his workers' astonishment, Greg openly declared the office as sacred at a monthly meeting and made them all accountable for maintaining the good vibes. While this may seem a little "New Age-y" for a CPA, he did this on the advice of the feng shui practitioner because she promised that he'd get better results from his employees if they saw their workplace as holy and kept up the good energy.

With nothing to lose and everything to gain, my client went along. In a few short months, not only did he fully recover the losses from his ended partnership, he was also able to expand his practice and add two new financial coaching services because the thorough work of his dedicated employees allowed him to expand into new territory.

You see, when you recognize your workplace as sacred and make it beautiful to reflect its worth, it begins to become a place where miracles happen. So why not see it as sacred? At its best, this is the area that supports your basic needs, fosters your creativity, introduces you to new people, and allows you to contribute to the world and find your personal power. It deserves to be respected and treated as a place you honor and value.

People who don't value working in a pleasant atmosphere are often very five-sensory and quite miserable because of it, while those who value their spirit will want to take it to work in a lovely place. If you have to go to a dreary workplace, you're going to become dreary yourself.

The more beautiful the workplace, the better the vibes and the more positive everyone will be. It makes a huge difference in your workday experience—and in your bankbook as well.

Your Turn

This week, take pride in your place of work and commit to making it as beautiful as possible, filling it with good vibes. Look your best and add you own personal beauty to the mix by smiling and being bright, cheerful, and positive. Care about the place—put flowers on your desk (and perhaps bring some for the whole office), and keep your personal work area, as well as shared spaces, tidy. Do this because you take pride in where you work and consider it important.

In addition, bring in a talisman as a means of symbolizing that this is a sacred place. It can be a symbol on your desk or a shrine in your drawer. It can be a family photo or a picture of your favorite spiritual teacher. It can even be a scene from nature. Be creative—it's *your* symbol, so choose what works for you.

In your pocket notebook, record how infusing your workspace with good vibes has affected things. Did you notice a change because of your efforts? Did it help your day-to-day mood? Did it help business?

THE BOTTOM LINE:

View your workplace as sacred.

STRATEGY #6

RESPECT OTHERS

Six-sensory people understand that we're all in this game of business (and life) together, and that on a soul level, we're all made of the same essence: Divine spirit. We also understand that no matter what role people play on the outside, everyone is the same on the inside—as such, everyone is deserving of the same respect, appreciation, and consideration we ourselves desire to be afforded.

Five-sensories tend to define themselves and others by the roles they play, rather than connecting to people in a genuine way. Six-sensory, intuitive people, on the other hand, bypass appearances and always interact with people in a genuine, respectful, authentic way, or "soul to soul" as I say.

Connecting to people on this deeper level is a powerful tool in business and in life. There's probably little we crave more from others than wanting to be accurately seen and appreciated for who we are and treated in a respectful, caring way. This desire to be recognized beyond appearances, financial means, and social status is so powerful that we go out of our way for those who afford us such recognition and hold long-standing grudges against those who don't.

A Gallup poll that asked two million people what they valued most in a job found the top answer to be "feeling cared about and respected by" their boss and co-workers. Hence, the number one key to success is recognizing and dealing with people in a genuine soul-to-soul way, treating them with the courtesy and respect they deserve.

The forces of business may be dictated, above all, by what people value at any given moment, but feeling valued never goes out of style, and those who appreciate us never fall out of favor. Furthermore, most of us are pretty savvy when it comes to picking up on the true intentions of energy being broadcast toward us. We can tell the difference between someone showing genuine interest in us and someone using superficial schmooze to get something from us. Genuine appreciation draws us forward, gains our trust, and opens our hearts and eventually our wallets. Schmoozing, on the other hand, may flatter and entertain us, but it ultimately leaves us feeling manipulated and suspicious.

The most serious business error I witness over and over again—the one that costs more time, money, and endless frustration—is the habit of treating others disrespectfully and condescendingly. People who get snubbed want to get even: Employees will show up late for work or do a lousy job; employers will demote or fire you; clients will drop you like a hot potato.

If you're guilty of this, remember two things: (1) You'll never get away with mistreating another due to the laws of karma and reciprocity—remember that what goes around comes around; and (2) you'll always pay the price for arrogance.

My client Ralph owned an international manufacturing firm that specialized in making replacement automotive parts. He had more than 200 employees, dozens of whom traveled on a regular basis (Ralph was a million-mile traveler himself), so he gave his chosen air carrier thousands of dollars in business a year. One summer, after a particularly tiring series of meetings on the West Coast, he boarded his flight back to Chicago feeling weary and irritable.

As Ralph took his first-class seat, the flight attendants were engaged in a coffee klatch in the galley and failed to greet him. Minutes passed and no one took his jacket or offered him a drink. Observing their preoccupation, and feeling extremely thirsty, he got up and went to the galley. He handed his jacket to a young male flight attendant who was at the center of the conversation, and asked him for a glass of ice water.

The flight attendant, thinking that Ralph was being funny, rolled his eyes at the interruption and teased, "Why? Are you special?" to which they all laughed. Taking the jacket and jokingly handing him a Styrofoam cup of warm water, the attendant continued to hold court with the others.

My client quietly accepted the water and the slight and sat down, thinking, *No, I can see that I'm not special here at all.* The next day he moved his company's business to another carrier. The joke was on the flight attendant, as his airline ended up paying the price of disrespect.

This sort of psychic response to poor treatment isn't uncommon. My friend Billy Corgan, a well-known rock star who recently purchased a magnificent estate along Chicago's North Shore, set out, casually dressed, to furnish his dream house. Prepared to spend lots of money, he ran across a quaint antique shop in a nearby village and began quietly browsing its wonderful collection. The owner, talking on the phone, gave him the once-over and, apparently not approving of his appearance, curtly asked, "Can I help you?"

Taken aback by her unfriendliness, Billy answered with a wave that indicated he'd like to look around for the moment.

She responded with, "Please wait. Can't you see I'm on the phone?"

Billy walked out. A minute later, recognizing who he was, the proprietor ran after him and asked him to come back into the store. He declined, of course.

He then went to a shop a few blocks away where he was met with great enthusiasm and wonderful vibes, although the elderly proprietor had no idea who Billy was. He spent $25,000 on the spot and promised to come back.

6 WAYS TO RESPECT OTHERS

1. Greet those you meet with a warm, friendly smile.
2. Look people directly in the eye when you speak to them.
3. Be patient and interested when dealing with others, not rushed and irritated.
4. Remember people's names and use them.
5. Say thank you and mean it when you're helped, or when someone gives you their business.
6. Listen to others without interrupting.

As obvious as this seems, I believe that many people don't fully appreciate the profound importance of treating people, no matter who they are or how they appear, with the consideration and respect they deserve. Energetically speaking, no matter what you see on the surface, *every* human being is a Divine soul entitled to courtesy and appreciation. Six-sensory people know this—the sooner you realize it, the better your business will run. Anyone who refuses to shift into this awareness is remaining in the Dark Ages.

Your Turn

Take a good look at your attitude toward others: Are you respectful and considerate; or are you impatient, condescending, and rude? Do you treat all people with the same courtesy, or do you operate on a sliding scale in the manners department?

Being disrespectful is business suicide; being insincere is no better. People are perceptive and will feel your true intention, even if they don't articulate it. And if your intention isn't benevolent, they'll put up their defenses and withhold their creativity. All of this costs you money and opportunity.

If you're an employer, you set the tone for your entire business, so have enough confidence and courtesy to be respectful of your employees at all times. Don't let your insecurities drive you to knock down those who support you. If you want them to do a good job, treat them as important . . . which, of course, they are.

If you're an employee, treat your peers and customers with respect. Disrespecting them is like shooting yourself in the foot. Be kind and genuinely interested in your colleagues this week, taking the time to verbally appreciate them.

In addition to appreciating others directly, use your

pocket notebook every day to write down at least three things you appreciate about your co-workers, employees, and clients that you haven't expressed. Don't be stingy in your acknowledgments. Six-sensories know that we're all in this together, and the sooner you accept this, and appreciate those you rely on, the better—for your bankbook *and* your spirit.

THE BOTTOM LINE:

Be considerate and respectful of others.

STRATEGY #7

RESPECT YOURSELF

I once had a client, Pam, who developed a health-care program for a national advertising agency based in Chicago. Her wonderful team of talented female professionals had created a program that had the potential to become a national template for all corporate health care. One of the agency's senior veeps, an old-school fellow, took a very condescending and negative attitude toward them, perhaps because they were women, and he made little attempt to cover it up.

Pam was incensed at the man's arrogance, and she respected herself and her wonderful team enough to refuse to be treated that way. So, fully prepared for the consequences, she went over his head and announced to his boss that her entire team was prepared to take their groundbreaking program to another company if the man wasn't removed from the project immediately. He was summarily fired.

With this man out of their way, Pam and her team were able to turn their health-care program into a new national model that was embraced by dozens of other companies. Both the company and Pam's team enjoyed huge success.

As you can tell from Pam's example, the politics of power and control that have plagued the workplace for decades are rapidly collapsing as an accepted business practice today. In this new, more egalitarian and spiritually shifting world, the soul in each of us won't be diminished any longer, and those who continue to apply such five-sensory behavior to others wreak havoc on their business and themselves as people rebel. In every case, it causes people to close their minds—as well as their hearts and wallets.

If you want to be a six-sensory success, never think that you can slight another and get away with it. It's a mark of confidence, competence, clarity, and great leadership to extend equality, dignity, and courtesy to all; it's also the sign of an evolved person. And it will come back to you tenfold.

Start by having self-respect and self-appreciation so that you can extend it to others, especially in the workplace. People often unconsciously treat others the way they treat themselves. In other words, if you attack yourself with negative self-talk, it's all too easy to extend that criticism to those around you, often without realizing it.

I just returned from presenting a weekend workshop at an extremely beautiful resort where I'd had the pleasure of teaching before. Looking forward to returning, I was quite surprised to be greeted rather curtly by the director of events, a person with whom I'd enjoyed a wonderful rapport in the past. He was too busy to say hello and was outwardly irritated with my simple requests for making the teaching space feel friendlier, such as adding fresh flowers and water for the guests. He even snapped at me when I asked him to adjust the overheated room temperature.

Unsure how to react to his behavior, I chose to ignore it at first, but by his third rude comment I asked him if he was feeling okay because it seemed as if he wasn't quite himself. Surprised to be gently confronted, he told me he was having some troubles with his superiors, and his attitude had nothing to do with me. He was worried about his job and wasn't in the best of moods, which explained his rudeness.

I was the unfortunate recipient of this guy's internal negativity, which was caused by his preoccupation with his problems. I forgave him because I recognized that we all have our bad days, but if I hadn't had the previous positive experience, it would have turned me off from going to that venue again. It's important to remember that we project our internal emotional state onto others far more than we realize, and this is bad for business.

My client Regina was the manager of a small manufacturing firm in Cleveland. Having endured an abusive childhood, as well as going through a second divorce, she suffered a terrible case of low self-esteem. Since she'd been spoken to in an aggressive manner all her life, Regina was very defensive, and sarcastic to her employees. Although she was a good employer and worked very hard, her poor communication skills led most of her staff to view her as harsh, rude, and extremely condescending. She ignored most of the complaints against her until the day she was demoted to a lower position where she worked by herself. She was told that the number of complaints against her were too numerous to ignore.

Shocked, my client finally took some responsibility for how she affected people and began receiving counseling. Only after several months of self-examination did Regina realize how hard she was on herself and how she continued to abuse herself with the same negative self-talk she grew up with. When she eased up on herself, she found a new patience and appreciation for those around her. It took her two years to regain the status she'd lost in her company—but now she's extremely respectful of both herself and others, and her career is back on track.

7 WAYS TO BE SELF-RESPECTING

1. Don't overwork as a habit.
2. Be willing to walk away from any situation that compromises your integrity.
3. Ask for what you need in order to succeed.
4. Don't be self-deprecating when you receive some type of acknowledgment—just say thank you and smile.
5. If you're experiencing a high degree of stress or are feeling insecure, take a few moments to get centered and meditate before tackling the problem at hand.
6. Laugh freely and often.
7. Be honest.

If you have personal problems that are affecting your work, be mature and honest enough to address them on your own time. See a therapist or doctor, hire a coach, go to a 12-step meeting, join a church—do whatever it takes to feel good in your own skin and peaceful in your heart so that those you interact with will feel good in your company. That's a formula for success both on the job and in life.

Your Turn

Take a good look at your attitude toward yourself: Do you speak to yourself with patience, appreciation, and respect, or are you self-critical to a fault? People are perceptive—they'll feel your inner landscape even if you think it's a secret. If your energy is critical of your own self, it will seep outward toward others. Others will feel this, but often they'll misread it and take it personally—as a result, they'll put up their defenses and withhold their creativity, all of which costs money and opportunity.

If you're an employer, you set the tone for the entire business, so don't let your insecurities allow you to ever attack those who support you. If you want to succeed, be kind to yourself. This is more motivating than criticism any day of the week, for it also seeps out to others. The kinder you are, the more motivated others will be to do business with you.

Use your pocket notebook every day this week to write down at least three things you appreciate about yourself. Don't be modest; be truthful. Acknowledge your successes so that you're not dependent on others for recognition—this will build your confidence. Acknowledge your failures as well, but don't hang your head in shame when you make a mistake. Study your mistakes and learn from them, listing ways you can improve next time. Seek advice. Ask for help. Take a class to strengthen your knowledge and skills. Laugh at your mistakes and forgive yourself. The sooner you accept and appreciate yourself, the sooner you'll accept and appreciate others. This is good for business and will help things flow at work.

Also, make note of any occasions where you felt slighted by another, or where you received better-than-usual treatment: What was your reaction to either situation? Also, note when you might have been less than courteous to someone else. Write down how you were feeling about yourself at that moment. Be honest—it will only help you if you tell the truth and look at the results. Finally, look in the mirror and smile. This will help ease any bad vibes or challenges you face.

THE BOTTOM LINE:

Stand up for yourself.

STRATEGY #8

WONDER

Over the years I've encountered endless members of the "Woulda-Coulda-Shoulda Club" of missed moments and lost opportunities at work. For example, there was the trader who lamented that he failed to get out of tech stocks and into bonds (as his vibes advised him to) just before the dot-com implosion, thus leaving him bankrupt. Then there was the ad exec who, out of fear of change, turned down a headhunter's offer to interview at another company, only to be let go two months later when his account pulled its business. And let's not forget the clothing salesman who languished in regret for not starting an import company for Italian bicycle clothing in the '80s, only to see the fitness craze escalate off the charts in the early '90s. And the list goes on and on. . . .

When I ask people why they didn't follow their intuition, most say that they killed these notions by dismissing them as fantasy before they were even born. Unfortunately, soul direction from a higher plane is ignored all the time, yet you can't follow your vibes to greater things if you're constantly squelching your inner voice. You have to be open to intuitive guidance to benefit from it, especially at work. Great inventions, "lightbulb" insights, and grand solutions are free-floating throughout the creative ether, just like radio waves are being broadcast through space all the time.

Being open to your vibes at work invites your inner genius to the table. Rather than simply working to survive, which is fear based and debilitating, you immediately shift into working to create, which is soul based and energizing. This immediately turns any job into a far more productive experience.

The front door to your inner genius is marked "Wonder." The minute you turn your awareness over to that wonder, your mind steps aside and your intuition becomes activated. Wondering invites invention, adventure, and exploration of things to come. It shifts you out of defense and self-preservation and into creativity and collaboration with your Higher Self.

Often we're too busy trying to figure things out to allow ourselves the opportunity to wonder. Yet wondering taps in to our right brain (the creative side) and explores new possibilities and unknown variables, while figuring things out taps in to our left brain (the logical side) and draws from past experiences and known variables. Wondering seeks to expand; figuring it out seeks to control.

One of the best ways to fuel creative solutions at work is to let your imagination wander by wondering on paper. Try to spend a few minutes a day wondering in your notebook about your work challenges and obstacles. Also, whenever you get stuck on a problem on the job, just jot down the issue in one column and then use your imagination to quickly note as many solutions as you can possibly think of, however outrageous, in the other column.

Wonder as a sport, with the intention of discovering solutions as you do. Often this jogs the creative mind and quickly flushes out creative answers in no time.

I asked Meghan, a very frustrated apprentice architect who was grossly underpaid and overworked, to wonder about how she could best use her talents to advance her desire to have more freedom and make more money. Taking my advice, she wondered on paper every morning for a month. The answer that repeatedly presented itself was to leave her large firm and start her own business fixing up houses. Her wondering also suggested that she ask her brother, a talented carpenter, to work with her on the first project and get financing from her stepfather, a retired broker.

Not used to asking for help or collaborating with family, Meghan initially ignored these bright ideas, but they kept appearing on her wonder pages. So, on a whim at a July 4th family picnic, she broached the idea with her brother and stepfather. To her surprise, not only were they up for the experiment, but her brother even had a place in mind. They shook hands and set out to see what they could do. Lo and behold, just before they put the renovated house on the market, a vacant plot of land nearby was chosen for a new shopping mall—and the value of the house doubled overnight.

Six houses and a comfortable bank account later, Meghan and her brother quit their day jobs and formed their own firm. They now have a large construction company in Utah with more than 20 employees.

Remember that all great ideas begin somewhere—yours may be waiting to be born on the tablet right in front of you!

7 STEPS TO EMPOWERED WONDERING

1. Dialogue with your "inner genius" by naming it. It has a voice and wants to use it, but it's waiting for an invitation from you.

2. Check in with your inner genius often; ask it to guide you on specific work issues and listen to its response.

3. In your notebook, jot down what your inner genius has to say. Solutions arise from within, but we rarely think to look there, being conditioned to seek outwardly from others instead.

4. Whenever possible, wonder out loud. As you voice your options, pay attention to how each one resonates within your body. Verbally and energetically try on various solutions to see which ones (if any) fit.

5. Wonder with your clients about what they really want and aren't asking for (or may not even be aware of).

6. Wonder with co-workers about new ways to do the same old assignments.

7. Wonder with friends and family about new job or business possibilities.

When my client Tracy was faced with a sudden loss of two key staffers in his auditing firm due to inconsistent business, he wasn't sure if he should replace them, find a partner, hire temps, or just work 20 hours a day. He wondered out loud about each choice: Even though his brain liked the idea of hiring temporary help because the money was manageable, his body felt far more at ease when he voiced the idea of finding a partner. When he wondered what kind of partner best suited him, his inner genius clearly stated that an older, semiretired person with years of experience but not too much ambition would be ideal.

Tracy was open to this idea, but he wasn't willing to search yet. The first person the temp agency sent was a newly widowed accountant who was forced out of retirement by her husband's untimely death. Grateful for the opportunity, she excelled at the job and became a wonderful complement to my client. After 14 months, he offered her a limited partnership, which she gladly accepted. Working four days a week, she handles all new business, while Tracy develops existing clients and financial planning. It's a perfect partnership.

Before Tracy wondered aloud, he only focused on the problem—after wondering, the solution instantly appeared. You see, the solution to a work dilemma often lurks just below the surface of your awareness and simply needs to be mined through exploration. Voicing your intuition and paying attention to your inner genius puts you in the driver's seat of any work situation.

No matter what situation you face, whether at work or in life, there's always a solution. Five-sensory people, who tend to get stuck and frustrated on the job, are intimidated by their problems and wait for others to provide solutions. Six-sensory, creative beings are *inspired* by problems and obstacles at work and love finding their own solutions.

Your Turn

This week, use your pocket notebook to wonder about all your business challenges on its pages. Write down each problem and come up with at least a dozen solutions. Stretch your imagination muscles and let your ideas run free. If you can find a trusted friend, wonder out loud by using him or her as a sounding board. Listen to your solutions and feel the vibration of the various possibilities to see which, if any, feels right. And have fun while doing this! The creative and intuitive mind is also the playful mind. So don't get too serious about this exercise: Just let the ideas roll out and see what presents itself.

You can also wonder out loud in the shower or in the car, or wherever it's safe. Pay attention and expect solutions. One more thing: People have asked me if they can wonder on computers or laptops. I suppose you can try, but in my experience it never works as well. Experiment and see if you can get into as free-form a mode on your computer as you can with a pen. I can't, but you may be able to. At any rate, do what works for you.

THE BOTTOM LINE:

Life is full of wonderful solutions.

STRATEGY #9

BE DECISIVE

You may be the sort of person who has all the intuitive insights in the world and receives tremendous "Aha! flashes," bright ideas, and consistent and accurate vibes at work, but unless you embrace them for the gold they are—and then act upon them—they won't do you any good.

I talk to people all the time who torment themselves with psychic regret because they missed their moment and hesitated to follow their vibes. Rarely do I encounter a person who's totally blindsided in business by an unexpected turn of events. Even the dot-com implosion was intuitively anticipated by many, most of whom admitted to playing a glamorized version of Russian roulette toward the end because they ignored the vibes that told them to get out in the hopes of having one last infusion of cash before closing up shop.

I spoke to dozens of "Silicon Valley victims" shortly after their fortunes went up in smoke, and every one of them confessed to denying their intuition of impending doom because no one else seemed to share their feelings. Oh well, live and learn. . . .

Learn to listen to and trust your vibes—especially if others think you're nuts. No great business breakthrough that I know of was ever supported by the masses. "They" thought Walt Disney was crazy, and wrote the Wright Brothers off as cuckoo. The Beatles were considered a band with a stupid name, and were essentially ignored in Liverpool, while Bill Gates was dismissed outright as a geeky college dropout.

Being six-sensory in a five-sensory world, you'll rarely get a supporting consensus—so you'll just have to decide for yourself to listen to your gut and follow through.

The most common reason I hear clients hesitating is this: "How can I be sure it's a true vibe and not wishful thinking or fear?" The answer is: You can't. Your vibes alert you to a moving target of energy and can change at any time. What you *can* be sure of is that if you get a vibe, it's trying to tell you something and it's worth listening to, even if the outcome isn't guaranteed. You don't pick up on vibes for nothing, so there's something you need to pay attention to. The trick is to zero in on what they're trying to convey.

4 WAYS TO FINE-TUNE YOUR VIBES AND ELIMINATE CONFUSION

1. Start by going back to your breath—inhale and exhale deeply.

2. Check in with your body: Are you tired, overtaxed, in a hurry, or being pressured? If so, ask everyone to back off and give you some breathing room in whatever creative way possible.

3. Ask for a few moments (or even an hour or two) to ponder the problem before you respond or decide what to do, as this will gain you time. Just say that you make better decisions when you're clear, and you need a moment or two to get to that state of mind.

4. Next, remind yourself of your goals—establish once again what you hope to achieve. As I've said before, your intuition supports your true goals, so the clearer you are and the less pressured you feel, the easier it will be to tune in to your vibes to make good decisions.

My client Delores worked as a project manager at an educational publishing company. She had a very strong vibe to fire a staffer for her constant lack of productivity and her inability to finish projects on time. The woman, however, had been with the company for more than ten years, while Delores had only been a manager for a little over a year.

As a show of good faith, Delores gave this woman six months to improve. She did, but inconsistently. To make matters even more difficult, the woman was the boss's sister-in-law and was recovering from breast cancer—firing her could appear heartless, jeopardizing Delores's own job. She grappled with her vibes over the situation for weeks, clearly feeling that the woman needed to go, yet not wanting to be the ogre.

My first question for Delores was: "What are your goals?" She said that she wanted to build the best team the company had ever known and personally mentor each employee to be their individual best. I then asked Delores if she was doing both with her troublesome employee.

"No," she replied. "The team is compromised, and she's unmotivated and disinterested. She clearly can't stay here because it's not important to her. Even in our reviews she doesn't fight for her job."

"Given your goals, should you trust your vibes and fire her or not?" I inquired.

After a moment, Delores said, "Given my goals, my vibes say to fire her. It may even be what she wants. I'm going to do it."

The next day Delores let the staffer go with a handsome severance package. The woman took the news stoically, but smiled at the severance package. A week later, Delores's boss dropped in unexpectedly, saying that he wanted to talk about her decision. Holding her breath, but willing to stand behind what she'd done, she invited him in. To her surprise, he thanked her.

"We've been encouraging her to quit for years, especially after her bout with cancer, but she wouldn't hear of it," Delores's boss explained. "Not because she loved the job or even wanted it, but rather out of some misguided sense of loyalty to me. We're all happy that someone stepped in and stopped her from wasting any more time—hers *and* ours. I believe that she and my brother will move out west and pursue more fulfilling goals while they can."

Know that in every case of trusting your vibes, there comes a moment when you're going to have to decide which way to go. There are no guarantees, but there will be experiences that can serve as guidelines. Get into the habit of writing down your vibes in your small pocket notebook as they arise. Don't censor, edit, or argue—simply record your instincts and feelings and see what happens over a two- or three-week period. By this time you should see whether your vibes are reliable. The more you write them down, the more importance you'll give them and the more specific they'll become. In a few short weeks, your vibes will become more and more frequent and refined. The notebook provides a framework within which to judge.

My experience says that in three weeks you'll have concrete evidence that your vibes are worth following. Don't trust me; trust your notebook. When you're not clear on what to do, a piece of advice my mentors gave me seems to work: When in doubt, check in with your body. Go over each option or vibe and see if it leaves you feeling energized, relieved, empowered, calmer, or somehow satisfied. If so, chances are good that your vibe is accurate, so go with it.

However, if an option leaves you feeling disturbed, troubled, restless, antsy, nauseated, or dissatisfied, your intuitive wires may be crossed—so you should back off from decisions and give yourself a little more time. Go for a walk and let things percolate a little more. Sound out your options as you walk, and let them ring back to your own ears. Accurate vibes somehow manage to ring true, while crossed wires don't have the same vibrational impact. If it rings true, go for it; if it doesn't, leave it alone for now.

Your Turn

This week, write down every vibe, hunch, and Aha! feeling you get in your pocket notebook—and don't censor, edit, or figure out what they mean. See what happens over time.

Practice acting on your vibes in small ways: When the phone rings, announce who's calling before picking it up. When the mail comes, speculate what's inside before you open the box. When looking for a parking space, call out where one is as you approach the area. This way, you'll get in the habit of acting on your vibes every day in nonthreatening ways that are entertaining and have no negative consequences should they be wrong. Get used to taking small intuitive risks until you become comfortable . . . then the bigger risks can follow.

THE BOTTOM LINE:

Be decisive.

PART II

Moving Up

STRATEGY #10

TAKE A RISK

If there's any single factor in determining one's ability to succeed on the job, it's the willingness to take a risk. I've never known anyone who has achieved great professional success without taking chances along the way, yet this is precisely what scares people the most. Those who do risk are few and far between.

There are two camps in the work world—the five-sensory followers who play it safe, and the six-sensory leaders who "live it true." Followers prefer predictable outcomes, seek guarantees for their efforts, and avoid the unknown at all costs. They do what they're told, stick to the rules, know that their paycheck will be there every two weeks, and refuse to do anything outside this safety net. Leaders, on the other hand, listen to their hearts, trust their vibes, do what they feel, and take the risks necessary to follow their inner voice, even if it means giving up a regular paycheck and taking a chance on their dreams.

The basic difference between the two is that those who live it true take full responsibility for making their dreams happen, while those who play it safe do not. Followers rely on others to take care of their security, while leaders know that it's best to rely on their own hearts, talents, creativity, and work ethic.

While five- and six-sensories may display equal talents at work, five-sensories tend to be ruled by fear, insecurity, and low self-esteem; conversely, six-sensories are guided by courage and a valuable sense of self that leads them to entirely different outcomes. Those who play it safe are often frustrated and feel trapped, while those who live it true may be frustrated and even scared at times, but they never feel trapped. They keep seeking new ways to create what they really want to do on the job. And although five-sensories often confuse taking risks with being reckless, six-sensories understand that gambling is a necessary part of developing their personal power and authority.

I had a gifted client named Lee who was getting nowhere in his job as a copywriter for a New York advertising agency, so he wanted me to help him find his true path. I could see that his true calling was to be a freelance screenwriter, and I told him if he took the risk and made a dedicated effort, he'd eventually succeed.

Lee's face lit up, and he confirmed that it was indeed his secret dream to write for TV and film. But then he shook his head and said that even if what I told him was true, he felt that it wasn't realistic to try at this time to make a living by writing. He was newly married, and his wife was pregnant with their first child—they needed money and insurance, so he couldn't even consider being a freelance writer or he'd feel incredibly irresponsible to his family.

I responded that he shouldn't quit his job or be irresponsible in any way, but instead stop having such a "mental death grip" on his job and trust his talent. "Taking risks doesn't mean being a flake," I said. "It means having the faith to give your dreams a chance, one step at a time."

I went on to suggest that he keep his job as a temporary means to an end, but at the same time make a serious and consistent effort to complete at least one screenplay on the side. Even though Lee had the talent, and writing was his dream, he rarely sat down to do it—instead, he spent most of his limited free time drinking with his buddies and complaining about his job.

Consulting my vibes, I told him, "If you want to be a professional writer, you must write on a regular basis. Besides, the job you're so afraid to let go of is about to let go of you."

Surprised, he asked what I meant by that. I explained that I saw a series of layoffs at his work in the next few months, and he was going to be one of them. "Not again," he moaned. "That'll be the fifth time in three years!"

"My point exactly," I said. "Your conviction that a regular job is the safest way to security isn't being supported by the facts. Stop avoiding your true desire and talent and give it a chance to develop. Take any job that meets your basic financial needs, but at the same time, work every day on your screenplay. Put in consistent hours (even if it's only a couple a day) as though it were a real job, and see what happens in the next six months. You have nothing to lose."

Lee listened halfheartedly—unfortunately, his insecurity, as well as his attachment to a predictable paycheck, outweighed his desire to follow his vibes and trust his true calling. Sure enough, two months later he was laid off . . . again. He couldn't find other work anywhere in the advertising industry in New York. His baby was born, and he and his wife were forced to move in with her family in Cincinnati. Yet his job situation fared no better there:

He landed a copy-editor assignment but was soon laid off again.

In the meantime, he and his wife brainstormed business concepts endlessly so that they could get free of these constant setbacks. They came up with a hot-dog stand, a used-clothing store, even a New Age coffee-and-tea shop—none of which fulfilled Lee's dream of writing screenplays. After a year and a half of unemployment and low self-esteem, he finally found the courage to change course and roll the dice. As he said in an e-mail: "I've been clinging to the *Titanic,* afraid of the water, and I find that I'm drowning in my own fear. I've changed my mind and am going after my dream because as you said, I have nothing more to lose. Wish me luck."

Last I heard, Lee was working in Los Angeles on daytime-TV scripts. I don't know for certain if he's working on his screenplay, but I do know in my heart that if he is, he's going to succeed.

As I said before, taking risks doesn't mean being irresponsible, cavalier, or reckless; nor is it simply crossing your fingers and hoping it works out, although some of that is involved. It's actually quite the opposite. Taking a risk means being willing to do *whatever* it takes—morning, noon, and night; seven days a week; week after week; year after year—even when it's painful, while still having faith that your efforts will eventually pay off.

You needn't have blind faith—you just need enough to keep you going when all else tells you to stop. It isn't easy, but it can be done. And those who do go after their true desires on the job by trusting their vibes usually succeed. Not all people have the courage to give up guarantees, but those who have pursued their dreams and taken the risks required aren't concerned about guarantees. They pursue what they love and trust that their efforts will eventually lead to success.

Every dream you pursue is like a planting a garden—you till, weed, plant, water, and then wait for it to grow. Part of taking a risk is having the willingness to wait for the garden to grow—on its own time and in its way, not yours.

WHILE TAKING CHANCES IS NECESSARY for success, it's wise to prepare for them along the way. Being practical is important, as long as it serves your goals and doesn't hold you back. If your vibes lead you to pursue changes on the job—especially big ones that have no guarantees, such as changing careers or going freelance—it's a good idea to support them with a plan. In addition, having a plan can be the very thing that makes taking risks possible. You don't have to leap from tall buildings; you can simply take tiny, but consistent, steps into the unknown and still succeed.

For example, I work with a talented musician named Mark Welch who took a big risk 16 years ago when he decided to leave his job as a middle-school teacher to fulfill his dream of becoming a full-time musician. He knew in his heart and soul that it was the right thing for him to do, but he was frightened by the notion of getting started. He knew that he'd have to give up a regular salary to live the adventurous life of a musician, so he decided to ease his transition by preparing for it well in advance.

First, Mark decided to quit his job one year after his initial decision. Next, he saved every penny he could and put it in a savings account. He also cashed in his modest retirement fund so that he'd have a small nest egg to pay his bills if necessary,

Then, as a way of emotionally preparing for the unknown, he played a little game to help him get used to the future: Every time he came to a curb, instead of stepping off, he'd close his eyes and jump off to create the sensation of going into the unknown. As small and silly as this sounds, it helped smooth Mark's transition considerably. By the time he left his job, he'd stepped into the unknown so many times he could hardly wait. He was ready, he took the plunge, and he never looked back.

6 WAYS TO PREPARE FOR RISKS AS YOU PURSUE YOUR DREAM JOB

1. Make a plan.
2. Save money if you can.
3. Make certain that your talents match your desire.
4. Get emotionally ready by creating opportunities to take little leaps of faith.
5. Look forward with enthusiasm to your new adventure, and talk about it with excitement rather than dread.
6. Take small steps, and don't overshoot your goal.

When I suggest taking risks, especially about trusting your vibes, I'm not asking you to trust me. I'm telling you to begin to fully trust *yourself*. If you've been using your pocket notebook faithfully, you'll have concrete evidence by now that your vibes are trustworthy. And please know that the Universe is ready when you are: The more you take the risk of trusting your vibes and moving toward your dreams, the more the Universe will move toward you, meeting you somewhere in the middle. Those who take risks will tell you that this is true—those who don't will never know.

Your Turn

This week, write down all your dream jobs, fantasy wishes, and true heart's desires in your notebook. Jot down what risks you're avoiding: Where are you playing it safe instead of living true? Next, choose a first step in your professional-advancement plan and go for it. Note five things you can do to prepare yourself for risk, such as starting a separate savings account for the future, working at a weekend job in some field you love, creating new business cards with your ideal job printed on them, or signing up for a class to improve your skills in the field you want to work in.

To build up your emotional and psychic reserves for change and adventuring into the unknown, play chancy games, including the board game *Risk*. When approaching a curb, close your eyes and jump off. Walk backward with your eyes closed. Have someone blindfold you and lead you around the block. Dance with your eyes closed. In other words, practice giving up control and surrendering to the unknown. Record your experiences every day, and most important, write down how you feel when you take these small, calculated risks—and trust your vibes instead of your brain. If you like it, keep going. . . .

THE BOTTOM LINE:

Roll the dice.

STRATEGY #11

ACT LIKE A WINNER

The best-kept six-sensory secret for changing your vibration overnight and succeeding on any job immediately is quite simple—so simple that most people can't believe it, let alone even consider it. The secret is this: *If you want to succeed, act as though you're succeeding now.* That's right—act as if you are, at this very moment, attaining your heart's desire in your work.

Before you dismiss this, let me elaborate on why this simple strategy works. Scientists and metaphysicians alike agree that our experience is born out of our focused intentions, which represent the sum total of our imagination. When we imagine something to the point that we feel its energy, our focus begins to completely support it. And once our focus supports our imagination, it begins to drive our attitude, choices, actions, and creativity—all of which define our outcome. So those who imagine they succeed, do so, while those who imagine they won't, don't.

Imagination fuels action, which drives outcome. When you envision something, you give it a heartbeat and a life of its own. That's because the mind can't differentiate between what's real and what's imagined—to the mind, it's all real. Mark Twain observed this when he said, "A lot of horrible things have happened to me, some of which actually occurred."

Six-sensories take this wisdom even further by understanding that the personal experience is created by our thoughts. I like to take the old adage "As a man thinketh, so he is" a step further: "As a man *feeleth,* so he is." In other words, those who feel like winners are—but those who feel stuck and left behind also are.

My mom used to tell us as kids to invent new ways to be happy when we'd get bored and cranky. She'd even show us how she did it by acting silly, telling jokes, and making funny faces. Intrigued with her creativity, we'd join in, and before you knew it, we were over our doldrums and on to having fun.

The bottom line is that you can't create what you can't imagine; conversely, you always create what you do imagine. Donald Trump was once asked about his phenomenal success, to which he replied with a shrug, "Simple. I cannot imagine me failing." I can't imagine that of "the Donald" either. And that's another point: Those who act successful recruit others who treat them as such. By acting successfully, you build a psychic consensus that vibrationally attracts the confidence and support of even more people. As the saying goes, "Success breeds success."

I have a friend who's defied all the odds to become a movie legend. Incredibly talented though he is, I truly believe that it was his unwavering conviction in his power from the beginning, accepting nothing less from himself, that catapulted him to the top.

This kind of "as if" behavior is easier said than done when it comes to the imagination. I find that most people have extremely flabby visualization muscles. For example, I once suggested to a gentleman who was trying to create a Christmas-ornament business that produced handblown collectibles of well-known cartoon characters that he'd be highly successful if he stayed the course.

In my enthusiasm for his idea, I went so far as to tell him that he could possibly become the most renowned name in Christmas collectibles if he stuck with it. His immediate response was, "Oh, well, I can't imagine that."

Apparently not, for after a year or two, I never heard from him or his company again.

Also, keep in mind that you cannot imagine your success alone, especially if you're surrounded by people who envision the opposite for you. I've seen dream after dream dashed by the people closest to the dreamer. In their supposedly good intentions, these negative control freaks project their own soul-deadening imaginations onto other people's bright intentions, thus squeezing the life force out of them. So be aware: It's not enough to act successful, you must also take that decision a step further and surround yourself with others who believe in your dreams, and dream along with you.

Years ago, it was my all-consuming heart's desire (professionally, at least) to expand my teaching practice to books and become a writer. But try as I might, I simply could not see myself as a legitimate writer. This proved to be a self-fulfilling prophecy: When I gave my first manuscript to a freelance editor, her only comment was, "Is English your first language?"

Devastated, I stopped writing. Yet my dream was later resurrected when my friend Julia Cameron, author of *The Artist's Way,* asked me about my book.

"What book?" I asked, blushing.

"The one I see you'd love to write," she answered. "The one I'd love to read." No matter how much I tried to tell her that I wasn't a writer, she insisted, "I see what I see. You *are* a writer."

Her belief reignited mine. Soon my first book, *The Psychic Pathway,* was published, and I've been writing ever since. Without Julia's imagination working on my behalf, I wonder if I ever would have written that book. I doubt it.

Besides finding support from people who dream big with and for you, you can boost your imagination by learning from those who've gone before you. Read autobiographies of successful people, particularly those in your area of interest. Study them, observe their attitudes and behaviors (especially their choices and actions). Find out what they did to succeed, and follow in their footsteps. Act like they did and watch where it takes you.

Movies are another great way to amp up your imagination and get you geared for success. Watch "can do" films where the protagonists stay strong, faithful, and true to their intentions, no matter what obstacles or opposition they face, such as *Rocky, Chocolat,* or *The Man Who Would Be King,* which are a few of my favorites.

Also, try to capture the spirit of the main characters and imagine possessing that same spirit. When I was in high school, for instance, I saw the movie *7 Faces of Dr. Lao* with Tony Randall, and it instantly inspired me to travel the world and speak my truth without compromise like nothing ever had. To this day, I reflect on the inspiration I drew from that movie, and it still keeps me motivated and laughing.

Another great way to boost your imagination is to visualize your success as though you're watching a movie. For example, try a game of golf: If you have a 14 handicap, imagine it going to 10; if you have a 10, imagine it going to 8; or imagine a scratch game (no handicap). What are you wearing? How are you holding the club? At what point in your swing do you feel perfection?

I once read that every day for the seven years he was held in solitary confinement as a POW in Vietnam, Major James Nesmeth used to visualize his golf game for hours on end. He imagined playing golf to keep his sanity and preserve his spirit. The first time he actually played after he returned home, he shot an amazing 74, 20 strokes less than his previous record. It's like Wayne Dyer says, "You'll see it when you believe it."

From my experience, this is true: Imagination is the place where we decide to believe in ourselves. In our inner world, nothing holds us back or gets in the way but ourselves. There's no interference, and nothing can stop you. Even quantum physicists agree that our success originates in our imaginations. Those who see success create it; those who see failure also create it. It's up to you how you want to use your imagination, but however you use it, it will create exactly what you imagine.

ANOTHER WAY TO ACT LIKE A WINNER is to use your imagination to create a secret persona who embodies all that success means to you. I have my secret powerhouse whom I've playfully named "Zena, the Warrior Goddess" (not to be confused with Xena, Warrior Princess—as a goddess, my Zena is much stronger and far more competent than any princess could ever be). Zena is strong, courageous, fearless, and full of humor, unlike the me who gets nervous and scared and sometimes overwhelmed by too much energy; consequently, I incorporate her energy into every public speech I make. When tapping in to my inner Zena, I can address any number of people at any time, remain fully grounded, and thoroughly enjoy myself while doing so.

My low-key and somewhat conservative friend Cal followed my lead and created his own successful, dashing persona named "Duke Monsoon, world-class hotelier and host with the most." Laughing as I pried details from him, he told me that Duke was a combination of Donald Trump and James Bond. Liberated from his number-crunching thinking as a banker, Cal's Duke had no trouble opening a successful group of boutique nightclubs in Chicago and Miami that set a new trend in entertainment. By freeing his alter ego, he was able to access a natural confidence and flair for taking risks that rarely if ever manifested through his ordinary perspective and personality. By letting this more adventurous part of his nature flow, Cal made a fortune . . . and got quite a few dates as well.

7 TIPS FOR BECOMING A WINNER

1. Read autobiographies of people you admire.
2. Watch *The Man Who Would Be King* and *A Star Is Born.*
3. Name and liberate your secret alter ego, who is a champion of the world.
4. Surround yourself with people who are willing to believe in you and your biggest dreams.
5. Dress like a winner.
6. Without being obnoxious, talk only of your successes—present *and* future.
7. Plan on winning—and then imagine the celebration party afterward.

My teacher and mentor Charlie Goodman said it best years ago when I was just beginning to have professional dreams. He suggested that I regularly remember to "get over yourself and connect to your spirit." By that he meant that I shouldn't let myself get trapped by the personality I formed along the way to be safe, but which only clips my wings now.

Creating alter egos may feel silly to those who are firmly entrenched in their egos, but I assure you that it will rev up your creative engine, free your inhibitions, access your intuitive notions more readily, not to mention spice up your life. (Just look at Clark Kent and what it did for him!) Besides, it's the perfect way to get over yourself, get past your limitations, and connect to your spirit, keeping the best of what's possible flowing through you at all times.

Your Turn

This week, use your imagination to create a secret persona, and act as that person every day. Be the genius of marketing, the world's greatest salesperson, or an Academy Award–winning star. Be whatever captures your imagination—don't worry about pretending.

Describe your secret persona in your notebook: What does he or she look like? What's his or her name? What does he or she wear? What are his or her best traits? What's in his or her closet? What are your persona's secret tools for success? Using your notebook as a springboard for your imagination, envision this exercise as an invitation to become who you truly are.

Making two columns on a fresh page in your notebook,

write down your fears and limitations at work in column A; in column B, record how your secret persona would handle them. With the help of your secret persona, recognize your limitations and push through them. Have the courage to imagine big success, and if in doubt, fake it till you make it. Surprisingly, this works just as well.

THE BOTTOM LINE:

Get over yourself and spread your wings.

STRATEGY #12

DO YOUR HOMEWORK

Once you accept the wisdom of trusting your vibes at work, you must lay the foundation for them to work for you. Your sixth sense is subtle and often fleeting, and unless your attention is primed to capture it (even throughout your demanding workday), chances are that you'll miss its messages.

The first thing to understand is that your sixth sense doesn't replace or bypass your other senses, but rather works with them—especially your common sense—to give you the best picture of the situation at hand.

Often people erroneously believe that being intuitive eliminates the need to be informed. This isn't true. The best insights are built on a solid foundation of firsthand awareness—they're never random shots in the dark. The more accurately and fully informed you are about your job and co-workers, the better the chances are that your higher awareness will guide you toward ways to improve.

So the first step in priming your intuition at work is to become as knowledgeable as possible about everything to do with your job—assignments, coworkers, clients, problems, challenges, rewards, and so on. After all, the first definition of *intuit* in the dictionary is "to pay attention," while the second is "to notice." In other words, intuition isn't an act of tuning in to some otherworldly dimension, as some would have you believe; instead, it's the art of fully being aware of what's happening in front of you right now, and then following it.

Whenever my clients are faced with serious challenges or are devoid of direction on the job, nine times out of ten it's because they're confused or poorly informed. When I talk about being informed, I don't mean that you should just gather data (although that *is* important)—that alone does nothing to activate your intuition or juice up your business creativity.

Rather, I'm talking about being informed in a way that only firsthand experience in the business trenches—being up close and personally engaged with real clients, your fellow workers, and supervisors on a regular basis—can give. That's where the six-sensory excitement begins to hatch.

For example, my client John, a recently retired and quite wealthy stockbroker, had a sudden burst of intuition to purchase a restaurant in the Chicago suburbs to fulfill his dream of owning a trendy, upscale eatery. Although he was new to the food business, he was an enthusiastic gambler who wasn't afraid of a challenge, and he had the money and temperament to take a risk.

John found a great location, commissioned a beautiful interior, recruited an up-and-coming chef to create an exciting menu, hired two friends who shared his dream as managers, and opened for business. He thought that he'd covered all the bases and couldn't fail.

Despite his enormous enthusiasm, vision, planning,

and large investment, my client was plagued with endless problems in hiring and keeping good employees. He couldn't understand why they kept quitting. Well, while he saw himself as a sophisticated, creative, equal-opportunity entrepreneur trying to give people a chance to prosper, his employees did not.

I didn't either. I saw a well-meaning, overly ambitious, poorly informed man who had tunnel vision; who was too self-enamored, naïve, and arrogant; and who focused only on what he wanted and was too busy to listen to anyone else. He was completely unaware of what his employees faced or needed during the course of a day, and he never took the time to find out.

John scheduled shifts that were way too long, allowed no input or feedback on the menu, over-guaranteed the amount of tips, and didn't compensate for the shortage with salaries—no wonder his employees quit. His blind spot was taking its toll, his restaurant was losing its reputation fast, and he stood to lose his entire investment. This brought him to me.

I pointed out how little firsthand knowledge he had of his business because he rarely visited it. He never worked in the kitchen, waited a table, or cleaned up after closing; and he spent no time getting to know his employees or his customers. It was okay that he was a beginner, but it wasn't okay that he pretended to know what he didn't. Rather than roll up his sleeves and learn on the job, he stuck to his business plan and followed his dream from afar, hoping for some miraculous solution.

I advised John to solve his problems by performing every job in the restaurant for a few weeks and learning what was really going on. I also told him to schedule meetings to get close to his staff. He enthusiastically agreed, but I could tell that as the boss, he really had no interest in doing work he considered beneath him, and he feared that getting intimate with his employees would erode his power.

Instead, he went to business school at Notre Dame, getting his master's degree but losing his restaurant. In spite of all of the sound five-sensory business information he acquired at school, John's still confused about why he failed. It's simple: When his intuition told him to open the best restaurant possible, he left his heart and soul out of the plan.

6 WAYS TO KEEP CURRENT

1. Listen to your customers, co-workers, and bosses.
2. Observe everything and ignore nothing.
3. Get hands-on experience whenever you can because it's the best teacher of all.
4. Ask questions—it's a sign that you're interested in doing a good job.
5. Be constantly open and curious.
6. Know your co-workers and clients by name, and remember what they share about their personal lives.

Richard Melman, founder of the Lettuce Entertain You restaurant empire, and someone I had the personal good fortune of working with 25 years ago, knows the wisdom of doing your homework and staying current better than anyone I know.

Starting off as a soda jerk at a neighborhood soda fountain, Rich worked his way to the top of a mega-million-dollar business by doing every single restaurant job himself, from busboy to cook to maître d', and later making all his managers do the same without exception. He encouraged leadership from within by seeking direct feedback from all staff members on any subject relevant to improving their jobs. He created programs for employees to get therapy for better self-awareness. And he rewarded people who helped him learn and were willing to work their way up with the same care, commitment, and informed interest as he had, making many ordinary people very wealthy.

Rich's other brilliant intuitive move was to visit his restaurants regularly and brainstorm with all his employees on how to make the locations more efficient, attractive, and fun. This led him to one creative concept after another, growing one of the most successful international restaurant businesses in the world.

And Rich isn't the exception: I have many successful clients who have arrived where they are in business by using these same principles and practices. They know what the job requires as well as what the people they work with require.

Your Turn

This week, sharpen your vibes by paying attention to what's going on at your workplace. Listen to your customers, co-workers, and bosses; observe everything, ignore nothing, and get hands-on experience whenever you can.

If you're stymied about something, ask questions, which is a sign that you're determined to do a good job. Now, don't confuse asking for information with asking others to do your job because you don't want to take the time to learn or do it yourself. In other words, don't pass the buck. Ask all the questions you must until you're completely clear.

Sharpening your vibes comes from knowing your job to the best of your ability. It also means doing your homework and keeping your awareness current. So be constantly open, curious, and involved. The more you do, the more information your inner genius will have to work with to provide guidance and direction.

In your pocket notebook, write down all the new things you've learned by delving a little deeper into the work trenches. What were you not aware of that you're glad you know now? What insights did you discover as a result of becoming better informed? What new information about your employees, co-workers, or boss did you find out? What fresh inspiration has arisen?

THE BOTTOM LINE:

Keep current and keep connected.

STRATEGY #13

EMBRACE CHANGE

You can receive all the guidance, direction, and insight in the world from your intuitive channel on how to advance to a greater level of success, but unless you're willing to act on it and follow a new direction if necessary, it will do you no good.

The willingness to try something new and venture into unknown territory, especially when your vibes tell you to do so, is basic to six-sensory success. In fact, the very point of seeking intuitive guidance is so you can make better decisions and act on them when it matters, while still keeping true to your real goals. This may involve constant change and even daily course adjustment.

If you're resistant to the new, you slam the door on your intuition. The foundation of six-sensory living is the ability to respond to life, moment by moment, and go with the flow of the energies at hand. The more open you are to this flow, the more flexible and responsive you'll become to the call for change, and the more you'll stay the course of your highest intentions.

Business is a lot like surfing: It shifts, recedes,

reaches low tides, and rolls in high waves—the only thing it does consistently is change. That means that the surfer who can follow the ocean and go with the flow becomes a champion, while the one who rigidly applies one technique gets jettisoned on the beach.

The thought of venturing into unknown territory is frightening to most people and throws their survival instincts into high gear. Change in the five-sensory world signals one thing: danger. But that's only an assumption handed down from generation to generation, probably since prehistoric times. That belief may have been relevant when facing dinosaurs, but it only holds you back today. Besides, although change can feel as though you're entering a dangerous place, the truth is that by the time an alteration is called for on the job, you're already in an insecure place and need to do something about it.

Several years ago my sister Soraya was suddenly faced with the great need to shake up everything in her professional life, yet she didn't know what to do. A commercial designer for more than 20 years, she worked at the Sears Tower, where most of her clients were located. However, her business instantly dried up after 9/11 as client after client moved out of the building for fear of being the target of another terrorist attack.

To worsen my sister's fortunes, the economy took a nosedive, and the few clients she managed to save called off their plans with her, leaving her out of work completely. With high overhead and no business, Soraya was forced to let her staff of five go, move her office into her home, and begin pounding the pavement for leads on new projects—along with hundreds of others in her field.

Living off of a home-equity loan, she was desperate

for a solution because she feared going into bankruptcy. I could see that she'd come to the end of the designer road, and it was time for a big change . . . and fast. So I told her, "It's clear that you must start over. As hard as it is to accept, you've come to the end of this road."

"What shall I do?" she lamented. "I have no other skills, and it's too late to change."

It may have *felt* too late, but the reality was that she had no other choice. My sister did have one skill, however, that could lead her to a new line of work I knew she'd love more than anything; she just didn't see it. Several years earlier, she'd gotten involved (along with her ten-year-old daughter) in learning how to fly on the trapeze. It started out as just a fun way to connect with each other and exercise at the same time, but it turned into an incredible shared passion. They began going to swing on the trapeze three, then four, then five times a week year-round, and in that time they both became extremely proficient.

To make it even more interesting, Soraya fell in love with a trapeze catcher, a handsome and charming man from Colombia named Elkin. After a one-year courtship, they eloped. The three of them lived together in Soraya's small home, loving each other, but struggling to make ends meet.

"Start your own trapeze business," I suggested, following my vibes. "Call it 'The Leap of Faith Experience,' and market it to people who are in the same position as you: at the end of one road and afraid to begin another. Tell them that by taking a leap of faith on the trapeze, they'll get to practice venturing into the unknown safely."

Upon hearing my suggestion, my sister's entire being lit up with excitement, and taking a deep breath, she decided on the spot to let go of her design business and her old ideas of what she needed to feel secure. Wondering where to begin, her vibes told her to present her idea to professional caretakers, nurses, therapists, and healers—that is, the people who rescue others but forget to have fun themselves. The vibe was right, because within weeks the calls started coming in. Word of mouth spread the news like wildfire among chiropractors, nurses, and massage therapists—then it leaped over to hospitals and fund-raisers, and the money started to roll in.

In the first year, the company did a modest $40,000 in business without spending a dime on advertising. It wasn't a gold mine, but it was enough to continue. The next year they took in $75,000, and they're still expanding. More important, Soraya and Elkin are having an exhilarating, joyful experience transforming people's lives and helping them overcome the fear of change.

As you can see from my sister's example, it's never too late to change if you're willing. Giving yourself permission to embrace the new at any point in life is one of the most intuitive, intelligent, and powerful business decisions you can make. People who allow themselves to change, when it's time to do so, stay on top. Those who don't usually make themselves sick and unhappy.

We all grow and shift: What interests us at age 20 or 30 may not even be important to us when we're 40 or 50. And in case you didn't already know, your soul has its own path and destiny—and whether you like it or not, it's going to stay true to its path and may not necessarily follow the one you mentally decide to take. If it's time for your soul to grow, you can feel it in your bones, even if your brain refuses to acknowledge it.

Of course, it's scary to venture into the unknown, but what's far scarier is to stay in the known if it isn't working, or to try to stop the winds of change when they bear down on you. That's an absolute guarantee for failure.

Your Turn

This week, keep open and flexible to change by modifying your routines each day. Take a different route to work. Sit facing a new direction. In your pocket notebook, write with your other hand. Ask questions when you normally remain silent; if you normally talk, listen. Mix up your wardrobe. Keep your life fresh and out of a rut. Record each new thing you did in your notebook, along with the serendipitous events that occurred as a result of your explorations and experiments. See how many entries you can make.

View change as sport, and pay attention to what happens as you cooperate. Especially notice the gifts that come with the new (there are always many). Follow what works, and let go of what doesn't—fast. My teachers always emphasized that change is a sign that it's time to make things even better, so look forward to it!

THE BOTTOM LINE:

Change with the times.

STRATEGY #14

GO FOR THE ADVENTURE

My teachers taught me that when you breathe into fear, it turns into adventure. Adventure appeals to your sense of wonder, your inner child, and most important, your creative self. It also reminds you that *you* make new things happen—the world doesn't just happen to you.

Embracing change requires this same kind of inhalation and expansion of imagination. If you take the passive view and perceive change to be nothing more than submitting to things that happen to you, you'll become a victim of your own lack of creativity and will get left behind. Instead, when something new is called for, view it as your invitation to adventure. Recognize it as an opportunity to express more of you, not less. And when changing, expect the Universe to favorably endorse, guide, and support your expansion.

Several years ago I spoke with a woman from Ukraine who'd emigrated to the United States shortly after the fall of Communism. I asked her if it was difficult to survive in her country after everything the people had counted on for the last

50 years came to a screeching halt.

Surprisingly, she shook her head and said, "No, not really. It was far too exciting to be a problem. Of course, there were those who did not want to change, but for the most part these people were dying anyway. The rest of us were challenged and eager for the opportunity. Never before were we so creative and motivated with new ideas. Suddenly everyone had an idea to make money, some more ludicrous than others—but most of all, we were happy to try something new. This was a pleasure we never felt under the shroud of Communism. It restored our life force and renewed our spirits."

If you work in a traditional setting, speak to your co-workers about embracing new things as an adventure and an opportunity, not as a doomsday event. If you're the one who's asked to change, take it on as something that's challenging or even entertaining. And if you're a boss and see that your employees need something different, include them in the process. Ask for their input, and have them stake a claim in the solutions you seek. The more a person is invested in something, the more open, creative, and intuitive they'll be in accepting it.

I know what I'm talking about here. As an ex-flight attendant who's maintained friendships with airline people for more than 30 years, I've witnessed multiple professional tragedies when my colleagues refused to accept change, even though the industry demanded it.

When the airline I worked for was taken over, hundreds of us were suddenly out of work, some after as many as 30 years on the job. It was terrible, but it was what it was. The ones who couldn't accept that their old life was over and couldn't move on to new things suffered the most. Several people had heart attacks, many more became severely depressed, and some even committed suicide.

Those who rigidly clung to memories of the airlines before deregulation (when they were paid well, worked little, and had a lot of time off) spent miserable years living in the past; resenting their jobs and hating their companies; hurting themselves, their co-workers, and the customers; and infecting everything with their bitter, angry energy. But the ones who were willing to accept and embrace the changes created fabulous new lives: Many took their extensive years of travel and public exposure and started fresh, some found new careers with other airlines, and many more created new businesses of their own. A lot of these individuals even admitted to me that they were far happier and more prosperous away from the cloud of fear that their old jobs had blanketed them in over the years.

The bottom line is that you don't have a choice when change is upon you, but you *do* have a say in how you respond to it, either negatively or positively. It isn't the world insisting that you transform as much as it is your own soul, which wants to grow and continue to bring all its creative gifts to the world. Whenever a transition is called for, view it as your soul knocking at the door of your life, bearing more gifts for you to bring to the world. You may have to dig for those gifts, but they're there.

THOSE WHO RESPOND POSITIVELY TO change engage their sixth sense in the process, and in doing so, directly connect to their intuition. Six-sensories accept that all things are constantly in a state of evolution, and they know that change is simply a spiritual reminder to evolve even more.

If the new scares you, write down the last time you were faced with significant change and how you survived. (You obviously did, or you wouldn't be reading this now.)

Ask yourself what positive things came out of that time: What intuitive experiences and synchronicities did you encounter in the process? What gifts did the Universe bring you? Were you open enough to accept them? Also, think back on the time or energy you might have wasted resisting change: What good did it do you? What was the effect on your health and peace of mind, as well as those around you?

Engage your sixth sense directly when you're faced with the need to change at work, or even change the job itself. Ask your Higher Self why this is all happening, along with what benefits you might gain from this situation. Voice your answers aloud if you can. You often intuitively know far more than you realize, and by talking things out, you'll give your inner self a voice. Better yet, ask a trusted friend to interview your spirit and pose these questions directly to it. Rest your logical brain and talk to your creative intuitive brain instead, and ask it to guide your transformation.

If you're an employer, engage your employees' imaginations by creating a safe atmosphere in which they can creatively discuss and ponder alterations on the job. Have them interview one another on what needs to change, and then listen to each other's answers. Rather than impose anything upon them, ask them to create changes with you as a joint venture. Have everyone contribute, and be willing to rework your plans several times if necessary as you experiment with new solutions.

Above all, know that change is a call from the soul to grow, and a catalyst for your creativity to flex its muscles. Be open to being guided to better solutions when new things become necessary. Listen very closely to your vibes as you move through this time, and keep the drama to a minimum. Who knows what wonderful adventure is waiting for you just behind your fears?

Your Turn

This week, make it your business to indulge in at least three to four new adventures. Break up your routine and go for it! See your world with fresh eyes, as if you're on vacation in your own backyard. Go to a new ethnic restaurant on the other side of town. Invite people you've just met over for dinner, or hit a karaoke bar and sing your song. Take a skydiving class or visit the new museum that just opened. Go for a run or a bike ride even if you feel that you're too old. Attend a rock concert featuring a band you've never heard of, or attend a play at an avant-garde theater. Take a red-hot sports car for a test drive.

Step out of your familiar and comfortable rut and try something daring. In your pocket notebook, write down all the new adventures you've allowed yourself to experience this week.

THE BOTTOM LINE:

Remember that life is as adventurous as you make it.

STRATEGY #15

HAVE THE COURAGE TO STAND ALONE

Making the decision to follow your vibes, even when those around you advise the contrary, takes courage and deep commitment. It's not easy to tune in to your inner radar amid universal doubt, particularly when your vibes point you in an unpopular direction. Yet not trusting your sixth sense, especially during work, will always—and I mean *always*—come back to haunt you.

For example, my client Gillian was a venture capitalist in Chicago. Recently out of grad school, she was contacted by a newly formed group, headed by a very aggressive woman, to launch business ventures in China that promised millions in revenue. Flattered to be considered and fascinated with the project, Gillian jumped at the opportunity. She loved China, raising money and the potential it promised, the group of guys involved, and being a pioneer—but she didn't love the leader, a woman whom she described as "the devil herself" for no other reason than the extraordinarily bad vibes Gillian got from her whenever they met.

Even though the leader was charismatic, charming, and stunning in her powers of persuasion, Gillian nevertheless felt that every time they spoke she was somehow being deceived and manipulated; however, she could never put her finger on how, nor did she have proof that her vibes were right. So my client—who could also see that her feelings weren't shared by her colleagues and was seduced by the company's potential for making millions—kept her vibes to herself.

Gillian tirelessly raised capital for the company and even took several trips to China to woo partners for potential joint ventures, but her bad vibes persisted. Finally unable to keep them to herself, she shared her feelings with some of her more trusted colleagues. Some laughed, while others were shocked, but not one of them agreed with her. Feeling isolated and uncertain of her vibes, she carried on, hoping that they would subside. They didn't.

Two years later, after ignoring every intuitive red flag, Gillian received a certified letter announcing that the company had been dissolved, bankrupted by the underhanded manipulation of the unscrupulous leader, who had absconded to Greece with the company's funds.

Stunned, but not surprised, Gillian didn't know whether to laugh or cry. What bothered her most was her willingness to ignore every instinct that advised her against working with this woman. The greatest reason wasn't the promise of sizable wealth—it was the fear of being laughed at or discredited by her highly educated, highly respected male teammates for questioning the ethics of the woman in charge. "When I received that letter," she told me, "all I could feel was that it served me right."

When her partners, who so readily dismissed her vibes, received their letters, Gillian did laugh out loud, reminding them of how they had shut her down. One of them, a highly esteemed Chinese-American financier, admitted to Gillian that he'd feared she was right in her assessment, but he'd naïvely decided that what he didn't know wouldn't hurt him.

To add insult to injury, four years later Gillian and all of her partners were named in a lawsuit by the investors they recruited. I wished her luck.

Another client, Rita, also had an experience involving great psychic regret. A self-made woman, she took great pride in being one of the top Realtors in the Kansas City area over the past 30 years. In addition to her impressive sales record, Rita was also proud that every one of her clients had had a positive, successful experience with her company and never registered a complaint against her, resulting in impeccable reputation—not a small thing in the real-estate business.

Deeply loyal to both clients and employees, Rita was caught off guard when one of her most trusted and longtime saleswomen asked for a special favor: She wanted Rita to hire her new live-in boyfriend as a salesman, since he'd recently gotten his license and needed a job. Normally, Rita wouldn't have hesitated because she was always open to hiring new sales representatives, but somehow this fellow gave her bad vibes, sight unseen.

Not wanting to disappoint her best employee, Rita shook off her vibes and hired the boyfriend. She even went overboard to welcome him into the company. On some level, she felt that if she was extremely nice to him, any negative feelings she had about him would simply go away.

He started out just fine and even closed a respectable number of deals in his first few months, so Rita wondered if her vibes had been wrong. Too busy to bother, and perhaps unconsciously looking the other way, Rita gave the man little scrutiny. All seemed well for about a year, but then disgruntled buyers started to file lawsuits against Rita. Apparently, her employee had sold houses with clauses for repairs and then arranged for unqualified contractors to do the work, who gave him kickbacks for the referrals. The repairs were faulty, and the victims were suing Rita for fraud.

Rita immediately called her salesman, but he and his girlfriend—whom Rita had employed and trusted for years—had skipped town. Disgusted with herself for letting her sentimentality override her vibes, she settled each suit without a fight.

Both Rita and Gillian ended up paying what we six-sensories call "the fool's tax," or the stiff penalty one always pays for not trusting one's vibes. The challenges these women faced in having to make the choice to trust their vibes over other pressures are classic: They both had the potential of being perceived as unprofessional, unintelligent, and even superstitious. It's understandable why they didn't follow their guts and took the easier road (easier for the moment, but not in the long run). What they failed to assess was the price they might have to pay for ignoring their vibes—in both cases, that price was thousands of dollars and lost reputations.

My point is that to be a truly six-sensory worker and leader, you must be prepared to take on difficult situations and follow your vibes all the time—even when you're asked to make unpopular decisions. Going with the consensus versus following your vibes may seem safe and prudent in the moment, but I've never once seen this decision prove to be smart in the long run.

5 WAYS TO SHARE YOUR VIBES WITH OTHERS

1. Present what you feel in a nonconfrontational way—just quietly make it known that these are your feelings.

2. Open the door for others to add to your vibes, without reacting unfavorably if they don't.

3. If you feel negatively toward a person or situation at work, frame your position in a question such as, "I feel a little hesitant about this. Does anyone here know why that might be the case?" Or, "Although this looks great to me, there's something a bit unsettling about it that I can't name. Does anybody have an idea what it is?"

4. Invite everyone to share their vibes with you. Even if they don't agree with you, at least they'll feel invited to open up.

5. After you state your feelings, open up the floor for comment (but never for approval). This prevents you from entering into a me-against-you dynamic, which never yields positive results in any work situation.

When it comes to trusting your vibes, you'll no doubt come to a fork in the work road where you're going to have to make a choice. Trusting your vibes may not be easy because you stand to be judged and misunderstood by your peers, clients, and bosses—and you may not be considered a team player if you don't go along with the program. But that doesn't change the fact that your vibes are there for a reason: to protect you, to maintain your integrity, and to lead you to the best possible outcome in every situation.

You'll have to decide whether to go along for the sake of temporary popularity and peace, or to be true to yourself and trust your vibes. Take it from me, it's not such a difficult choice. I encourage you to summon the courage to follow your sixth sense at all times, even though we live in a five-sensory, me-against-you world. It's a challenge worth undertaking, especially if you want to avoid becoming a regular dues-paying member of the "Woulda-Coulda-Shoulda Club" of work regret.

The best way to remain true to your vibes is to stay in touch with other six-sensories who share your convictions and will back your decisions. Six-sensories don't do well as the Lone Ranger, especially at work—we fare far better in clusters of kindred spirits who empathize with our challenges and support our intuitive perceptions and choices. And I've noticed that when we stick to our intuitive convictions, people will generally accept our vibes—and though they may not like them, they'll respect us for following them.

"But what if I'm wrong?" I can hear you asking, especially if you take a public stand on something difficult. Well, even if your vibes prove to be less than 100 percent accurate (which happens because vibes *can* be fickle sometimes), in almost every case I've observed it doesn't matter. What does matter is that when you demonstrate your courage in standing up for yourself at work, you'll be respected by everyone. And even if you aren't, you'll be respected by the most important person of all—you.

Your Turn

This week, claim your vibes and stick with them. Don't seek consensus or approval; instead, have the courage to listen to your sixth sense and trust it enough to let it be known. Practice writing it down in your notebook before you speak, as noting your gut feelings will help reinforce them. (Besides, writing down your vibes is a great way to fine-tune them.) Then act on what you feel. If others disagree, they have the right to do so. Just know within your deepest self that your vibes will guide you in your present job and will lead you to the best future ones.

THE BOTTOM LINE:

Stick to your gut feelings and convictions.

STRATEGY #16

BE AUTHENTIC

One of the most powerful decisions you can make in business is to be authentic. Simply put, this means that what you say, mean, intend, and do . . . agree with each other at all times. People who choose to behave in this way have a powerful healing vibration that commands respect and engenders trust, laying the foundation for success in any endeavor.

For a lot of people, the thought of being real is far too risky. Believing that who they really are isn't good enough, they spend all their time and energy trying to impress others by being what they think others want, instead of being themselves. Fearful of being discovered, they hide their true feelings and act defensively, leaving their spirit unavailable and their creative and intuitive energies blocked at the door. Yet despite their best efforts, this behavior simply doesn't work.

Being someone you're not is unnatural, time- and energy-consuming, and dishonest. It takes too much of your focus, as you continually try to restrain anyone from getting close enough to see through your façade. It isolates you from the flow of life, leaving absolutely no room for you to access the higher vibrations of your creative, instinctive self. And you're not fooling anyone: People are pretty intuitive, and they know a phony when they meet one, often because it takes one to know one. So in the end, all this posturing is a colossal waste of time that gets you nowhere.

Learning to be real is the greatest secret to success. Six-sensories know that who we really are isn't defined by our background, our personality, or even our education and life experiences. Although these things do influence our behavior, each of us is simply a beautiful Divine soul who's here on Earth to contribute our gifts and share our beauty. It may take years of counseling and therapy to accept this if you come from an unsafe family history, and it can be even more challenging if you struggle with active addictions. Being scrambled in the chaos of an addictive or phony vibration will sabotage any professional goals you have. (I don't want to discuss addictions in depth here, but if you do have them, it's imperative that you get real enough to address them and clear them up, or your dreams and goals are doomed.)

Accepting and being who you really are is the only way to truly succeed. The first step toward doing so in the workplace begins with keeping your word no matter what. Nothing empowers you more immediately than being a person who does what you say you will, with full integrity. When you give your word, people believe you—and if you follow through, they'll believe *in* you, aligning their vibrations with yours. When this happens, you gain their confidence, trust, and support; and in the end, you'll get their business, which is ultimately important for success.

However, understand that keeping your word goes well beyond just the literal interpretation of your agreement.

It's one thing, for example, to show up for work and then merely occupy your chair while your mind wanders all over the place, and it's quite another to truly be present—mind, body and spirit—and ready to do your job.

Five-sensories tend to focus only on the surface of life, pretending that only what appears is real *(I'm in the chair . . .)* while ignoring the deeper truth *(. . . but my brain is at home)*. Six-sensories, on the other hand, acknowledge what is more profoundly true *(My body is here, but my mind and spirit are absent)* and seek to be present on all levels at all times.

THE UNIVERSE IS CREATED BY SOUND and vibration, so words have tremendous power. When your spoken word resonates with your deeper intentions, it becomes a formidable force of attractive energy that commands attention, respect, and results. When you speak from such an empowered place, not only do others believe you, but the Universe believes you as well. Being a clear channel of integrity and intention, you get out of your own way and allow the Universe to flow through you and work on your behalf. When you establish this kind of integrity, the minute you say something, the Universe will rush in to make it so. Before you know it, your words will attract the very things you speak of right before your eyes.

I've seen this happen a thousand delightful times. For example, several years ago my husband and I intended to move and began looking for houses, starting in one of our favorite neighborhoods. As we walked by a particularly attractive home, I looked at him and said, "I want that one." I meant it, even though the houses in that area rarely went on the market, often being snatched up before anyone even had a chance to see them.

Six months later, I suggested that we walk by the place again. Just as we were approaching, a For Sale sign went up in front—one hour later, we signed a contract. Coincidence? No. It was the power of the word in action.

The person who keeps her word is the most secure person on the job. Her vibration is such that people count on her; she's the one they trust, support, and invest in. Having the vibration of integrity lends a power as impressive as any talent, skill, and education—maybe more. Such a vibration is business insurance, guaranteeing that doors will always open for you.

Exciting things happen when you consistently keep your word. You become so energetically empowered that you can call things forward by simply saying so. For instance, an oncologist client of mine, a man of impeccable reputation, used the power of his word to heal his patients on a regular basis. He told them, "Together, with God, we're going to turn this around if that's your intention." And he meant it.

His intention and vibration to heal were so clear and so high, and his commitment to do everything in his power to help his patients was so unyielding, that one after the other, he turned desperate, dying people into vibrant living beings once again, thus becoming a legend in his field.

I once asked him how he succeeded so often. His answer was: "I intend it, I say so, and I accept nothing less—not from me, not from my patient, not from God. By His grace, it simply works."

Businesspeople who have the vibration of personal integrity are often perceived by others to be lucky, but their "luck" arises out of their high intention and creative expression. Not only do they keep their word, they also use their words directly and creatively to attract exactly what they want. Listen closely to highly successful people: You'll often hear them often repeat statements such as, "We'll do it!" "I'll handle it!" or "I'll make this happen!" And they do.

My client Burt is a real-estate developer, and he's had so many successes in brokering one huge deal after another throughout southern Florida, in good economic times and bad, that people have actually written articles about his luck. He himself has even thought that he was operating under a lucky star.

A millionaire many times over, no matter how large or unlikely the deal he was working on, Burt consistently said, "I'm going to make this happen. I'm not sure how, but I will succeed." And then he did. The interesting thing is that Burt is just an ordinary guy with an extraordinary ability to work with impeccable integrity and focus, to do what he says he's going to do, to be real throughout the process, and to claim his success in advance through his intentions and words. He means what he says and he follows through (as does the Universe). When you talk to Burt, you can just feel the genuineness in his vibration.

Sadly, most people don't possess this kind of focused, authentic integrity. Their energies are scattered, leaving them spinning in circles. And their words reflect their internal struggle: They break commitments, distance themselves from their obligations, pretend that they didn't give their word at all, blame others, and complain to hide their lack of integrity. Then they wonder why their careers (and often their lives) are dead in the water. This may sound harsh, but it's more true than not.

People who are genuine work by the sweat of their brows as opposed to browbeating; set their intentions and honor their commitments, even when it's not easy to do so; and use their words truthfully and carefully to attract success. People who don't maintain this kind of clear vibration, no matter how convincing their reasons, will not succeed in the same way. That's because the laws of the Universe dictate, "As above, so below. As within, so without." Clarity begets clarity; confusion begets confusion.

When you get real, your vibration becomes very powerful. That's because the real you is a Divine being, empowered by God to co-create with the Universe. The Universe will work *with* you, but it won't work *for* you.

Have you ever heard the expression "God helps those who help themselves"? Well, it's true. By having the integrity to honor your word by your actions, you'll create a compelling vibration that flows with the Universe. I call this vibration a "state of grace," businesspeople call it "being on a roll," and five-sensory people call it "luck"—but whatever you call it, the results are undeniable. You become the most attractive, charismatic person on the job, with the ability to draw the opportunities and support you seek to you.

Your Turn

This week, pay attention to your commitments and agreements with customers, clients, co-workers, employees, and employers: What are you promising them? Are you fulfilling these promises? Completely? Are you telling the truth and keeping your agreements, not just literally, but in the full spirit of the agreement? Are you being genuine and careful in doing what you say you're going to do? If not, ask yourself what's preventing you from being real and honest. Whatever it is, it's very expensive, costing you a peaceful and successful life.

Write down your commitments in your pocket notebook, and also note any time you miss a commitment or let someone down. Sometimes we aren't fully aware of the holes in our integrity unless they stare back at us in black and white.

Clean up your act if necessary, and clear up your commitments if they're unfulfilled. Respect your words and know that they'll respect you. Use them to support, not sabotage, you, and you'll pave the way to success.

THE BOTTOM LINE:

Be real.

STRATEGY #17

ASK FOR HELP

One of the most powerful tools you can utilize for activating your intuition and getting your vibes working for you on the job is quite simply asking for help. By that I mean that you need to open up every door and window to your heart, mind, and imagination to let your Higher Self and your peers, colleagues, and bosses—in other words, the entire Universe—assist you in realizing your goals.

Asking for help is difficult for five-sensory people because they live in a paradigm of "me against you" where admitting vulnerability is threatening. Six-sensories, on the other hand, know that as spiritually connected human beings we're all in the game of life together, and when we ask for aid, we support each other and everyone benefits.

One of the most exciting breakthroughs in quantum physics is the affirmation that we're all spirit, and by letting spirit direct us by asking for help, we unleash the powerful potential to create anything we want in life. Requesting assistance isn't a sign of weakness, it's a sign of wisdom—especially if you're a leader. I often remind my clients that some of the greatest leaders of all time achieved their goals by first asking for help. Even Jesus asked for 12 helpers before he began his mission.

Six-sensories know that the door to success opens inward, beginning with acknowledging their limitations and not condemning themselves as incompetent. Yet when I suggest to clients that they open up and ask for help on the job, they often think I'm crazy. The mere thought of letting others know that they could use support makes some people uncomfortable and defensive—a classic five-sensory posture.

Just today, my client Ruth, a single woman in her early 50s who's managed a large health-care facility for the past 30 years, demonstrated a classic case of defensive misery. Her job is her life, and she does it well; at the same time, Ruth is very reserved, and she's been feeling uninspired and isolated of late. It was clear that she needed to reach out to others for inspiration.

Working long hours (sometimes six and seven days a week) and feeling like a fish out of water among the mostly younger married employees with children, my client had hidden her loneliness behind a guarded demeanor, never opening up to anyone. I suggested that she ask her boss to help her overcome her obstacles on the job.

Ruth gasped in fear. "I'd never dream of even thinking about such a request! It makes me extremely uncomfortable."

"Why?" I asked. "What does asking for help mean to you?"

"I'm not sure, but apparently it's not something I care to know."

"Einstein once said, 'Nothing changes if something doesn't move,'" I responded. "It's time to move off your present perspective and consider opening up to new influences. Just ask yourself what you're so afraid of."

"I'm afraid of being vulnerable," Ruth admitted. "And the thought of that isn't acceptable to me."

"Asking for help," I replied, "is not the same as being needy. It simply means that you have the wisdom to open up to new input when facing a challenge.

"And if you're truly open," I added, "it empowers both you and others. They get to connect with and contribute to you, building positive relationships that lead to great business. Consider it and see what happens."

Ruth was skeptical, but I encouraged her not to dismiss the idea. Just a few hours later, she called to excitedly report that when she returned to the office, her boss had asked how she was. Instead of giving the usual plastic smile and pat answer, she replied, "Truthfully, I'm not so great. I could use your help if you have a minute."

That led to a conversation with her boss that was very open and honest. Ruth confided that she felt isolated and uninspired and needed something new to get her remotivated on the job. Her boss acknowledged these feelings and said that she, too, had gone through a similar period. She offered to send my client to a progressive health-care conference in Las Vegas, just to get her thinking in a new direction. She also told my client that she'd pay the tuition if she wanted to pursue a master's degree in counseling, something Ruth had wanted for a long time, but never had the courage or resources to pursue.

Just by taking a chance and opening up to help from her boss, my client received two major surprises . . . then she burst into tears. Her boss laughed as she handed her a tissue and told Ruth that she'd been a great worker and that she was glad to further her career. "Don't ever hesitate to ask me for help," she said. "I'll do anything for such a solid employee as you."

I've learned over the years that the biggest reason people don't ask for help as often as they should is because they don't think it's an option. They've long been entrenched in the "do it by myself" culture, and they're so buried in their jobs that they don't even know what kind of help they need.

This is especially true of entrepreneurs, who are used to doing things on their own and in their own way. The idea that another person's way could be better doesn't come easily to them. Sure, doing things by yourself works up to a point, especially if you're self-employed, but eventually those strategies become a hindrance when you want to go further. You hit a ceiling, and unless you let others help you, you stay there.

I personally learned this the hard way. Years ago when my practice was small, I answered the phone, booked my appointments, arranged all my workshops, carried all my materials to and from the classroom, and did all my own bookkeeping. For a long time this worked, but when I began to write books, do public speaking, and conduct workshops all over the globe (in addition to having a couple of children), the demands of my job expanded my life beyond reach.

I found myself buried alive and feeling resentful about my work. It took a friend to suggest that I hire assistance both at the office and at home. At first I regarded the idea as a impractical novelty—but when I accepted her advice, I started to enjoy my work and my life again. I'm sure I would have become burned-out if I hadn't.

It's important to view asking for help as an empowering tool, both for yourself and others. You cannot be a control freak. A free-flowing attitude of give-and-take establishes trust and support, laying the foundation for taking risks and eventually achieving greater gains. The more we share our talents, the more creative and intuitive we become—and the more prosperity we'll achieve.

Agreeing in theory that it's a good idea to ask for help, a client who was a computer programmer for a large financial institution in Paris bemoaned that every time she asked for assistance, it inevitably failed, doubling her workload. It wasn't the first time I've heard this complaint.

You see, from an energetic perspective, this tendency often stems from an unconscious desire to maintain control, causing you to ask for help from someone who isn't qualified or competent. By doing this, you create a vicious cycle of believing that you can't trust anyone but yourself, thus driving you deeper into a corner. When you're ready to receive help, you'll stop this disappointing cycle and begin to recognize that real support is available, and engaging it won't make you small. In fact, it's empowering.

One of the laws of the Universe is "ask and you shall receive." The key is to be open to accept help when it does appear, especially if you're chronically overcompetent.

4 WAYS TO ASK FOR HELP—AND SUCCEED

1. First approach those who you're sure can aid you.
2. If you can't find anyone yourself, ask your colleagues if they can suggest someone to assist you.
3. Next, ask the Universe at large by saying aloud, "Help!"
4. Be as clear and specific as you can about what you want. People fail to get what they need when they don't know, or don't accurately communicate, what they seek.

I had a client named Magnus who'd just started a career as a freelance marketing consultant when she was hired to assist the Chiquita corporation in a time of transition. She was told it was a two-week job, but soon after she arrived, Magnus saw that the man who commissioned her was buried alive in work and needed quite a bit of assistance. So, when Magnus finished her assignment, she asked if there was any other way she could be of help.

Her client was so struck by the offer that he asked if she had any ideas . . . and she had plenty. For Magnus, that two-week assignment turned into a 15-year position, all because she offered—and he accepted—her help.

Six-sensories know that the Universe is ready, willing, and able to assist anyone at any time, but nothing happens until we ask. Five-sensories spend an awful lot of time acting as if they don't want or need anything, fearfully bluffing their way through their insecurity, putting out negative vibes, and keeping others at bay because they're afraid of being "found out." It's far more honest and efficient to speak up quickly when you don't understand something or are in over your head on the job, which is what six-sensories do. They spend little time struggling with a challenge—instead, they do everything in their power to eliminate confusion as soon as it shows up. They work from a collaborative approach and leave room for everyone to contribute and feel important.

The best six-sensory practice is to begin each day by asking the Universe for assistance. Mine is, "Divine Source, help me to be open to support, to do things the most efficient and creative way, to receive assistance from all sources possible, and to recognize new opportunities. Help me to learn, to appreciate and be appreciated, to prosper, and to enjoy my job. I am open to all forms of help and all means by which you send it: Surprise me."

I say this prayer when I shower, my friends say versions of it as they walk though their office doors, and others say it while they drive to work. Voice this prayer yourself, or make up one of your own to state every day before you begin working. The more you say it, the more you'll create an opening for help from your Higher Self and your intuition.

During the day, every time someone asks if you need help, instead of saying "No, thanks" say "Yes." If you're unclear about how they can assist you, ask if they have any ideas—and then listen. Whenever you feel stuck on the job, look up and to the right, which accesses your intuition, and say "Help" out loud. Then take few deep breaths and back off to allow the ideas to flow into your awareness.

Practice asking at least three people a day for aid until it feels natural. Try saying, "Can you lend me a hand? I could use some assistance. Do you have a moment? Are you available? Can I take a minute and ask you for some input?" and so on. Do this exercise, and help will fly in.

I just held a workshop where I invited each student to stand and ask the Universe for assistance. One woman said that she was starting a foundation to provide housing for the elderly, needed financial support to get it going, and would welcome any contribution. Before she left that day, she got $200,000 in pledges from the class.

Another woman wanted help in moving to Chicago and getting work. She received several job offers, as well as moving assistance. A third wondered how she could go about contacting a producer in Los Angeles to read her screenplay—she was immediately given the name and phone number of a producer from someone who'd known him for more than 20 years.

All three were very surprised at the responses . . . but I wasn't. In fact, one of my best friends, a marketing and finance specialist, received the best job offer of her life from a gentleman sitting next to her on a plane. She said that she liked his vibe immediately, so she decided to be cordial and strike up a conversation rather than ride in silence (which is what she normally would have done). My friend told this man about her job and how unhappy she was there. By the end of the flight, he offered her a position with his company, which she accepted.

I know that the Universe is always striving for your success, but *you* may not know it. Right before your eyes are more opportunities than you can imagine. You never can tell where help will come from, but know that it will come if you ask for it—and not a moment before.

Your Turn

Follow all the suggestions in this chapter in asking for help this week. In your pocket notebook, write down every request you make of others, how you made it, to whom you made it, and the results. Notice how the more you ask for aid, the more it comes. Make a list of those areas in your job where you'd like to receive assistance. Make two columns in the notebook: In column A, put down what you want; in column B, note what showed up.

Practice asking aloud for help when you're alone as often as you think of it—ask the Universe, your Divine support system, your Higher Mind, the Powers That Be, and your super-conscious mind. And write down the prayer for help that you'll use to start your day.

Six-sensories know that the Universe is there to support you and that you get what you ask for. So ask for a lot.

THE BOTTOM LINE:

Ask and you shall receive.

STRATEGY #18

FOLLOW YOUR HEART

The most basic six-sensory rule for succeeding at work is to follow your natural pleasures and passions and do what you love. Period. No exceptions.

No matter what anyone tells you, if you pursue what brings you joy, then half the battle for achieving success is already won. If you love what you're doing, you'll take yourself as far as you can go; if you don't like what you're doing, however, you won't be taking yourself anywhere.

Like a train running on its track, going after what's in your heart puts you in flow with your spirit. Pursuing what doesn't capture your heart, no matter how competent you may be at it, will never flow with your spirit—instead, it will deteriorate into a painful and resistant endurance test. Energetically speaking, working at something you don't enjoy disturbs your vibration, demoralizes your spirit, and sets you against yourself. And on a practical level, no matter how much you ignore it, doing what doesn't interest you will never bring you satisfaction or success of any sort, no matter how you rationalize it with your fears.

In the five-sensory world that's managed by fear, control, and the voices of others, doing what you love is dismissed as immature, unrealistic, and even irresponsible. Five-sensory people will discourage you from trusting your Divinely appointed interests and passions, telling you that you're never going to make it and that it's not practical. Most common will be the question of how you're ever going to pay your rent. The best response to five-sensory discouragement is, "How do you know that what I want to do won't pay the bills? You've never tried it."

Despite all the rhetoric to the contrary, anyone who's succeeded will tell you that the most important factor of their plan was simply this: They liked what they were doing, so they stuck with it and it worked out. You see, for success, you must be practical above all—and practically speaking, if you aren't enjoying yourself, you're on the wrong track, traveling a dead-end road and assuring your failure.

You can't succeed at anything if you aren't authentically engaged, and that can only happen in your heart. Never mind what others say, especially if they're discouraging—give no heed to any effort meant to cause you to doubt yourself. Any genuinely heartfelt interest pursued faithfully has the potential to make money, but far more important, it has the ability to guarantee satisfaction. That's what success is all about. Look at my sister Soraya and her trapeze business!

It's possible that by the time you reached the age when you had to work and support yourself, you'd been fed so much baloney and poor information that you doubted and second-guessed life . . . and now you've lost touch with what you care about most. If that's the case, you must take baby steps by remembering victories of the past.

My client Javier worked for 15 years as a hospital administrator, a job his mother got him straight out of college, and he hated every minute of it. I suggested that he move out of his job inertia by remembering his victories and the happiest moments of his life. In every instance, he was involved in sports: soccer, baseball, lacrosse, swimming, and track. Remembering how much fun he'd had until he was 16 filled Javier with a sense of enthusiasm and satisfaction that he hadn't felt in ages. Back then he'd envisioned himself playing pro sports, but then he was told that he didn't have what it took to be a professional. Defeated, he went into health care and psychology.

Accepting that at age 31 he certainly was no longer destined for pro soccer, my client decided to reconnect with his true love and volunteered to coach a girls' inner-city soccer league. He once again fell in love with the game and the world of sports. He kept his day job, but soon his life was consumed with sports, and he'd never been so happy.

Within two years Javier became volunteer head of the league. Continuing to have fun, he accepted a job offer as athletic director of a very prestigious private school. Now he's teamed up with several other sports enthusiasts, and they've decided to open a used-equipment store for kids who can't afford expensive top-of-the-line products. Just by remembering what he loved, and trusting it enough to follow that trail, my client has become a huge success—not just financially, but in his heart as well.

Your Turn

This week, list any successes you've had in the way of recognition, merit, awards, and bonuses. Go as far back as you can remember—most great people became that way by remaining faithful to what they loved when they were young. Next, write down every time you can remember having so much fun that you laughed until you cried: What were you doing? How did you feel? And would you call it a success?

These two exercises should give you some real clues about the direction your heart wants to go. Follow them before your inner control freak gets in there and stops you.

THE BOTTOM LINE:

To thine own self be true.

STRATEGY #19

MAKE NO ASSUMPTIONS

One of the most invaluable skills you can develop in any business is the ability to accurately perceive people—be they employers, employees, or customers—before you proceed with working together. The better able you are to intuitively dial in to their true intentions, needs, and objectives, the more effective, efficient, and ultimately prosperous your business relationships will be. After all, business at its core is simply the art of good relationships, which are based on having a solid sense of who people are and what they need—and then assisting them in reaching those goals.

Learning to accurately perceive people in business is both an art and a skill. The skill comes from developing a keen sense of observation and listening to what's present over what you're projecting, especially when it comes to what's motivating others. The art is in accurately interpreting your experience so that you draw proper conclusions, which then lead to better decisions.

The first ingredient in perceiving a person accurately is having a keen desire to want to know who that person is and what they want from you. Believe it or not, most people take very little genuine interest in the individuals they work with—they're far more focused on themselves and their own agendas.

I was recently reminded of this when I began to look for a new office space. Calling several commercial Realtors to whom I was referred, I was struck by the fact that most of them spent very little time getting to know me. Yes, they all asked the obvious questions of where I wanted to locate, the size office I was seeking, and how much money I wanted to spend, but they seemed to care little about who I was, what kind of atmosphere I needed to work in, and what sort of building appealed to me.

Two of them were so presumptuous and impatient, in fact, that I could barely answer their questions without being cut off, which annoyed me to no end. I felt completely invisible by the end of both conversations and decided before I even hung up the phone that I wasn't interested in working with either of them.

The third was slightly better, asking a few personal questions, but instead of listening to me, he kept saying, "I know what you mean" or "I know what you want" before I could finish my sentences. Clearly he *didn't* know me or what I wanted or needed at all because he wouldn't take the time to listen to find out. Twice when I was trying to explain what I was looking for he put me on hold and took another call. The third time was the last straw: I hung up, and he never called back.

Only the fourth person I contacted successfully connected with me. She didn't ask any of the usual questions until the very end of our conversation, focusing instead on who I was, and listening intently to what I was seeking. She wanted to know what mood I wanted my space to convey; what kind of light, size, and atmosphere I was seeking; and what general area I hoped to locate in. She even asked me what kind of vibration I was looking for—was it corporate, artsy, or something in between? She told me that the physical particulars of what I was looking for, in terms of size, dimension, and so forth, were easy enough to find. Discovering what my spirit was seeking in a professional work space was the greater challenge.

Needless to say, I went with her. We're still looking. It's taking some time, but I'm committed to staying with her until we find the right space because she "gets" me and is working hard to support my true desires. In the meantime, due to her diligence and desire to support my spirit, I've referred several new clients to her.

When it comes to accurately perceiving people, my mentors and teachers taught me to never assume that I really know anyone—not even those who are familiar with and close to me. After all, who people were yesterday is not necessarily who they are today or will be tomorrow. I've found that to be sound advice. More than any other business error, the most damaging one I've witnessed over the years is thinking that you know someone and then approaching that person based on your presumptions rather than reality.

Call it projection, call it transference, call it whatever you want—in my world, I call it a big mistake to assume you know someone to the point where you stop listening and paying attention to what's in front of you regarding that person today. If you work from old impressions, faulty conclusions, or stories you've made up about the person instead, this can (and will) cost you time and money.

The tendency to make false and premature assumptions is driven by three other gross business errors: impatience, sloppy observation, and arrogance. Rather than taking the time to genuinely learn about and connect with the person in front of them, most people tend to rush to conclusions based on superficial exchanges, appearances, past experiences, or hearsay—then they proceed to judge and project according to their own hasty and faulty observations.

For example, I consulted with Marjory, whose husband had recently died of a heart attack, leaving her the sole owner of his huge plastic-container-manufacturing company. Marjory was big, blonde, whiny, and nervous—at first glance, you'd think that she was incapable of managing her checkbook, let alone running a multimillion-dollar business. And that's exactly what her husband's attorney and family assumed. Consequently, they immediately set their agenda, which was to offer my client a quick buyout. Spearheaded by her husband's CFO and friend of 20 years, this group was sure that they'd be able to get Marjory out of the way with little resistance.

Little did they realize that my client was much more competent and committed to keeping her husband's business alive and well than appearances would indicate. Sensing his physical vulnerabilities well before his serious health problems appeared, Marjory had quietly been learning the business from him for several years. In the process, she discovered that it interested her a great deal, and although her husband kept her from actually participating while he was alive, with him gone, she was at least emotionally prepared to step in and take over. And what she didn't know, she was willing to learn as she went along.

Marjory shocked and dismayed everyone with her intentions, but it didn't matter—she'd made up her mind. Not reading her well, the company officers and their attorney tried very hard to dissuade and even block her from taking over; determined, she fired those on the old team who didn't support or respect her, and she went on to build a new one. The first two years were bumpy, but she managed to keep control as sales regained ground. To this day, Marjory is hanging in there. The fired officers are still trying to find legal ways to regain control of what they lost—so far, they've failed.

Keep in mind that you should never assume that you know everything about your co-workers either, especially if you're assuming the worst. This reminds me of my client Carlo, an intuitive young man who worked for a small but aggressive marketing and advertising agency. When he came to me, he complained bitterly about the other members of his team. "I'm a very open-minded, intuitive, creative man—a true six-sensory," he said, "yet I'm working in an extremely five-sensory—no, *four*-sensory—world. You don't dare share anything deeper than a saucer with them; they're that shallow. If I told any of these goons about my intuition, I'd get laughed out of the office, so I don't."

Sensitive to Carlo's dilemma, I invited him to attend a one-day workshop on six-sensory awareness that I was offering later that month. Delighted, he agreed. But when he arrived, he wasn't prepared to see that three out of the six members of his team were also at the workshop. Stunned, Carlo saw that maybe they weren't quite so shallow after all, and maybe it was *he* who wasn't reading things accurately. We both laughed at his mistake.

6 WAYS TO IMPROVE YOUR PERCEPTIONS

1. Throw all your assumptions and projections out the window and meet your world, and the people in it, with fresh eyes every day.

2. Avoid asking people their opinions on others before you meet them.

3. Be curious and patient—learn about others' perspectives and motives before drawing your conclusions.

4. Forget the past and deal with people in the moment.

5. Listen with an open mind and heart, and be willing to be surprised.

6. Don't compare people with others or believe that someone you meet today is just like another person you knew in the past.

My teacher and mentor Dr. Tully once told me, "Never assume you know anyone." That has proven to be sound advice in my life. People are changing and learning and growing all the time, even you. The person you were ten years ago, a year ago, or even last week is definitely not the person you are today. The same goes for other people.

Also, keep in mind that people aren't the same with everyone. If individuals feel judged, they'll likely be defensive and guarded, thus negating all creative potential; whereas if they feel safe, it will bring the best out in them and your possibilities together. By approaching people without preconceived notions, you leave the door open for positive, dynamic, and creative interactions that will be totally overlooked or shut down if you enter with a closed or judgmental mind.

A case in point is my husband, Patrick. When I met him, a lot of people who knew him told me that even though he was a likable guy, he was a flake, and I shouldn't give him the time of day. A world traveler who hadn't settled down yet, Patrick was perceived by others to be too transient to emotionally invest in. However, I was attracted to his cosmopolitan interests and adventurous spirit, so I ignored this well-intended advice and trusted my direct experience with him instead. I'm so glad I did.

We were married after a year of dating, and 21 years later, we're still going strong. Thank God I didn't listen to those who "knew" him.

Your Turn

Every time you interact with someone this week, check your judgments and stories about them at the door, and instead engage with an open heart and mind. This even applies to people you know, and especially to those with whom you've had challenges or difficulties in the past. Avoid conversations that tend toward gossip or second-hand opinions about others, and listen to "experts" with a discriminating ear. Don't carry others' projections into your encounters, thus sabotaging any creative potential you may have together.

Above all, trust that the Universe has brought you together for a reason. Be at your best, and expect the best from others.

THE BOTTOM LINE:

Never assume that you know anyone completely.

STRATEGY #20

GET A GOOD READ ON IT

Besides paying attention and observing everything you can, if you really want to master perceptions at work, you must learn to get a good read on people before you make your business decisions. To do so you must consciously notice, remember, and give importance to everything you observe and feel. For example, if you see someone shift when asked a particular question in an interview, notice it. Better yet, write it down as soon as you can. Ask yourself how you felt about the shift and write that down as well, and continue until you're in the habit of acknowledging these minute matters.

Do this with all types of subtle information: If you see someone clear his throat, write it down, as well as the question he was asked before he did so. If you observe him shifting his eyes—that is, looking to the left or right instead of straight at you—jot this down as well. Doing so will allow you to reflect on your impressions later when you have a private moment; if you don't, you may forget important clues that can influence your decision.

If you're clearly not a note taker or are in too much of a hurry to write things down all the time, a small tape recorder may be used to capture your impressions just as easily. The point isn't so much how you record your impressions, but that you do.

Simply observing without somehow acknowledging your vibes is not enough to fully hone in on what you pick up. It's far more effective in fine-tuning your vibes to outwardly acknowledge them in some way so that nothing slips by. The easiest way to do this is not to write down or record, but rather to share your observations with a trusted colleague or friend, someone who's neutral and can simply listen to your vibes and help you sort out what you're feeling. As you discuss your feelings with another person, don't be surprised to discover that you observed a lot more than you thought you did.

My client Audra was looking for a location to open an upscale clothing boutique. Having succeeded in another city, she wanted to open a second one in Chicago. She was shown a perfect location in a neighborhood that was right next to two planned, 80-story condo developments. The Realtor was extremely enthusiastic and couldn't have done a better job of selling her on the neighborhood, assuring Audra that it was the next hot spot in town.

Judging by appearances, his vision seemed a little optimistic, but he *was* convincing. Best of all, since it was a developing neighborhood, the rent was affordable, especially if my client signed a ten-year lease. And, he said, the planned condo development promised what could be a steady stream of customers right in her backyard.

When Audra came to see me, she'd pretty much decided to go for it—she only had to give her agent a call to seal the deal. And yet, as we talked it over, she became more and more hesitant. Three times she said, "I hope those condos go up as I was told," which gave me reason to pause. I asked her why she questioned it.

"I'm not sure," she reflected. "It's just that the guy was far less energetic when he mentioned those condos than when he talked about the neighborhood. To tell you the truth, I had a fleeting vibe that it wasn't such a sure deal on the condos."

"Do you still have that vibe?" I wondered.

"Yes, I really do."

"And if the condos don't go through?"

"Well, then I'd be risking a lot more. Too much, in fact, to make it a good location," she said, as if a lightbulb had just gone on in her head. "You know what? I can't do it," she realized aloud. "I was talked into it, but I can't. It's not right for me." Right then and there, she called her agent on her cell phone and cancelled the deal. She later rented a space in a suburban mall.

Two months after our meeting, 9/11 happened and the economy tanked. Audra's store survived, but those condos were never built. I believe that the Realtor knew they were iffy to begin with, which is what my client picked up on. Having talked it out with me, she was able to zero in on information she subconsciously registered but didn't acknowledge. Such a post-interview debriefing helps you access your vibes and make a better decision.

The next best thing to talking over your observations with a trusted, neutral (that's important) person is to simply voice your feelings out loud to yourself. You can also write down what you noticed along with your body's reactions. Your body is a huge energetic receiver, picking up on myriad bits of information, not all of it easy to remember or even register on a conscious level. As you write, be aware of the feelings in your body as you revisit the conversation.

7 WAYS TO PICK UP ON ANOTHER'S VIBES

1. Breathe in through your nose and gently out through your mouth as you take in everything about the person in front of you.

2. Notice their tone of voice, eye movement, body posture, mannerisms, words, and most important, defenses.

3. Notice their breathing patterns as they speak.

4. Listen deeply as you connect with them.

5. Begin to share a breath with them. As you do, you'll begin to synchronize your thoughts and perspectives with theirs.

6. Notice your body's reaction to what's being said: At any point do you feel disturbed or uncomfortable? Do you feel suspicious or tentative? Are you having any reaction at all? Despite their smile, for example, do you feel cautious? Despite their enthusiasm, do you feel turned off?

7. Take your time in making your observations, and *breathe*. Don't rush and don't project.

In addition to simply noticing vibes in general, it's especially important to be able to recognize what I call "red flag" vibes as well. These indicate that "something's wrong with this picture," so to speak—that is, if what you're hearing or observing is not the same as the real story. Paying attention to red-flag vibes can spare you a lot of regret later. These psychic signals alert you to the fact that someone isn't grounded, or that they're not as committed as they say they are, and this could leave you high and dry if you're not careful.

My client Leon, a rising star in the professional-speaking arena, was advised by several trusted friends to hire a certain well-known person in the field to be his manager. He was quite flattered to be considered as a client by this highly esteemed man.

Their initial conversation went well, and two more followed. Each time, the manager was quite enthusiastic about a potential business relationship with my client and didn't hesitate to say so, yet Leon wasn't sold. Writing down his observations, as I suggested, he noticed several red flags in their interaction. For one, he held his breath whenever the manager spoke, as though he didn't quite believe what the man had to say. Leon also noticed that the manager cleared his throat quite often when he spoke, which made my client uncomfortable, and he leaned away from Leon the whole time. Otherwise the guy was open,

10 RED FLAGS WHEN READING ANOTHER PERSON

1. Their jaw is clenched.
2. They're fidgeting.
3. Their eyes look away when you ask questions.
4. They're sweating.
5. There's an increased heart rate (yours as well as theirs).
6. They're laughing nervously.
7. They're coughing.
8. They're stuttering.
9. They lean away from you as they're speaking.
10. They give you a lukewarm or "cold fish" handshake.

My final suggestion for getting a good read on others is to take your time in making a decision. Reading people is tricky business because you must sort through a lot of information to get to the core and figure out whether you can create mutually satisfying and ideally prosperous outcomes. The worst thing you can do is rush your decision—so, as much as possible, reflect, review, and even sleep on it. Once the emotional content passes, your subconscious and Higher Self will deliver more clarity for making the right decisions.

You don't need much time: A day or two at the most is more than enough to assess your vibes correctly and get the right read. Take the time you need up front, and you'll save time in the long run.

Your Turn

This week, pay close attention to the people with whom you interact. Observe everything that goes on between you and what sticks out in your awareness most. Talk out these observations and see if anything else comes to mind as you do. Make notes in your pocket notebook after any significant conversation to help recall details that may otherwise slip your mind. Did you notice any important body language during your conversation? Did you get any uneasy feelings or positive vibes? Did you feel the person with whom you were speaking was being open, honest, direct, and fully disclosing? Do you share the same ideals and goals? Was there a natural rapport between you, or did you find yourself feeling on guard or trying too hard to make the shoe fit?

Write all of this down, and don't be surprised if more comes to mind as you do. Share your observations with a trusted, neutral friend and listen to yourself as you speak. Are you getting any new vibes by sounding things out loud? Take your time here—especially paying attention to any vibe you can't specifically define but that leaves you feeling vaguely hesitant or instinctively confident. Then trust what you get and go with it.

THE BOTTOM LINE:

Notice everything.

PART III

Rising to the Top

STRATEGY #21

WORK WITH THE RIGHT PEOPLE

One of the fundamental intuitive skills to develop in the business world is how to best select co-workers. Whether you're a boss seeking to hire a staffer, an employee looking for a job, a company about to select a consultant, or a self-employed entrepreneur hunting for new business, the need to work well with others is basic. According to Jim Collins, who wrote *Good to Great: Why Some Companies Make the Leap . . . and Others Don't,* the ability to make the right decision in choosing whom to work with is one of the deciding factors between success and failure.

If there's one area where your six-sensory skills can play a truly important part, it's in finding the right people to fill your work needs at the right time. Some of the greatest horror stories I've heard (and I've lived through a few myself) have come from not trusting vibes or getting an inaccurate read on a person or situation, and then connecting with someone who's a nightmare to work with.

But take heart: With a little refinement in your awareness and a serious commitment to trusting your vibes, you can hone your people-connecting skills. Even better, with more practice you can learn to use your vibes to directly summon the right people who will help take you to the top.

The first step is to be crystal clear about what you want from the connection. The more defined you are about your requirements, the more effective you'll be in attracting the right person for the job. Unfortunately, most people are less than 100 percent clear about what they need.

For example, let's say that you want to hire a front-desk receptionist, and you figure that anyone with good secretarial skills will do. Yet you overlook the fact that you also need someone who's empathetic, as well as a solid multitasker. Consequently, you hire someone who can type and answer the phone but who isn't particularly warm and can't do more than one thing at a time. So that person messes up regularly and quits after three frustrating weeks.

I can't stress enough the importance of *taking the time to focus on what you really need.* Think beyond "I need help" if you're hiring, or "I need money" if you're seeking work—instead, try to match the applicant or the situation with your intentions naturally.

Naturally is the key word here. Six-sensory people know that we're all basically set in our vibrational patterns, and either we're suited to something naturally, which makes us good at it and able to get better, or we aren't. People rarely change or become suited to something that doesn't resonate with their basic energy patterns. So if you find a colleague who matches you energetically, it's going to work out; if it isn't a match, it will never work out.

In high school, desperate for money, I took a job that was the worst possible match for my talents. Being compassionate and sociable, I found myself suffering at a desk in a sterile office above a men's haberdashery, posting monthly statements alongside the only other employee, an elderly woman who didn't speak to me. I was lonely and bored, deprived of using my natural people skills. During the third week, the posting machine suddenly started smoking and burst into flames for no apparent reason. But I knew why—I hated that machine (and the job) so much that I psychically torched it. I quit that day, before my boss realized that I was a secret poltergeist. He was glad to see me go, as was the other employee, who apparently had great talent for her job.

The point is that unless we energetically align ourselves with the right people and situations, we won't get very far. On a soul level, we're compelled to use our talents, and when we do we feel peaceful; when we don't, no matter how much money we make, we feel dissatisfied—and so will everyone around us.

On an energetic, intuitive level, correctly matching natural talent with task creates an energetic vacuum. The universe abhors a vacuum, so it will always seek to fill that void with whatever the void demands. Therefore, the more specific you are in identifying your void, the more specific the universe will be in filling it.

One more thing to remember: Avoid emergencies. Once you're clear about what you seek, be calm and relaxed as you go for it. Whether it's a job or an employee, no matter how urgent the need, avoid drama and stress. Stay grounded and take your time when seeking your match—don't rush your decision, and don't allow your search to become an emergency. I know that this can be difficult, especially if your bills aren't paid, projects are screaming for attention, and deadlines aren't being met and won't be until you get help. But trust me, *do not* allow your temporary situation to unground you or throw you into a state of emergency. You'll surely make poor choices that will only set you back further.

Intuition is best founded on the solid ground of reason and logic, so the more reasonable and logical you are about what you want in a person or situation, the better. Write down what the situation commands in detail and talk it over with others at work (if you can), or seek the counsel of a trusted friend. Be detailed and break down your search into assignments and what you need to do to fulfill each one. And as I've mentioned, don't rush. I learned this the hard way.

Several years ago my beloved assistant announced she was quitting and going back to school. For her, it was the right thing to do, and I supported her decision. But for me, it was devastating—and I panicked. To exacerbate matters, her departure couldn't have come at a worse time: I'd just released my third book and was leaving on a tour for it in ten days. Who would run the office? Everything screamed "Emergency!" and I was scared.

Instead of thinking it through and focusing on the talent I needed, I frantically called everyone I knew. When they asked what I needed, in my frenzied state I said, "Just someone who can answer the phone and who understands and loves people and my work as much as I do."

Well, I got what I asked for. The first woman I hired loved people and what I did so much that she started telling my clients I was too busy to see them—but she'd be happy to consult with them on my behalf at her home. The second person said he loved people, so much so that he began asking my clients, both male and female, out on dates. The third loved people and my work so much that she searched my computer, found my personal documents, stole my written work, and submitted it to publishers as her own.

How could this have happened to me, who's six-sensory and is supposed to know better? Didn't I have bad vibes about these people? Of course I did. I knew that each one wasn't a good fit. But, being in a state of emergency—and all too human—I ignored my vibes and rushed into hiring them. And I paid a terrible price.

When I returned from my book tour, I slowed down and examined my situation objectively. I realized that I really needed someone with the following qualities: (1) the patience to listen to people in emergencies; (2) a reliable work and moral ethic; (3) solid, professional boundaries; and (4) comfort in being the support person at the office.

I asked my vibes for help, and feeling unhurried, I put an ad on the Internet . . . and received 2,000 applications in three days. Remaining focused and grounded, I glanced through them all briefly—none felt right. Finally, I connected with someone through a phone call who sounded as grounded and calm as I now was. He said that he liked being of service, even though he had no idea what I did. He'd been a teacher before and loved supporting people and seeing them grow. And he had good vibes on the phone.

During the interview, he demonstrated the people skills (and ethics) I was looking for. It felt like a match, so I hired him. Six productive months later, we learned that one of my dearest and most respected colleagues and friends had been his boss and mentor throughout high school.

As you can see, once I was clear about what I wanted, I attracted the ideal support person, saving myself hours and hours of time interviewing the wrong people. Thus, the more grounded, clear, and focused you are in *your* intention, the more powerfully your vibes will point you to the right person.

Once you set a clear, focused intention, begin broadcasting what you're seeking. The universe will set about bringing it to you in short order. Try it and see for yourself.

Another tip: When interviewing, be open but detached, and breathe a lot. By that I mean that you need to listen to what's being communicated without trying to "make the shoe fit." Allow space as you listen. Remember, your vibes tune in to what *isn't* said as much as what is; silences are as telling as words.

Of course, you need to pay attention to the obvious as well: eye movement, manners, and enthusiasm. Most of all, see whether the intentions of the person or job you're considering align with your own—look for an easy verbal and energy flow. You'll know that the individual or situation is a match if you feel more energized and at ease at the end of your meeting than before it. Trust your vibes, despite what your logic says.

My client Chuck was seeking a new lead singer for his rapidly rising jazz orchestra. He clearly knew what he wanted as he auditioned people, and he was especially attracted to two women. One had a fantastic voice but made him feel uneasy. He couldn't put his finger on it and wondered if he was just being superstitious. The other candidate had a less powerful voice but had a wonderful vibe about her. He liked her ease and flow, her knowledge of the type of music he wrote and played, and her manner.

Confused, Chuck called me for advice. I suggested that he choose the one with the right vibe. I told him that he could improve a voice, but it would be a lot tougher to change a bad vibe. Yet, feeling insecure, he chose not to trust his intuition and hired the woman with the better voice.

What a mistake! She turned out to be a nightmare. A diva in her own mind, this woman had no talent what soever for working with other band members and saw them only as a means to serve her ego. She alienated everyone, sexually manipulated them all, and abruptly left for another band a few months later. Chuck felt like he'd been hit by a truck. He called the other singer once he recovered, but it was too late: She'd relocated to Nashville and was recording her first album with a new band.

Before making *any* decision, you should always sleep on it—that is, refrain from making a snap decision. Your intuition energetically registers every bit of information about a person or situation in the moment, but you need a little time to process that information and let it percolate before it can guide you. So take 24 hours to reflect on your vibes before you take action. This will provide enough time for the emotional impact of your meeting to wear off and the deeper connection to surface.

Alfred was a client who owned a couple of restaurants, and he wanted to hire and train new managers for potential partnership. He interviewed one who had stellar credentials, a terrific personality, and no limit on what he was willing to do for the company. Still, Alfred's vibes said, "He has ulterior motives—watch out!"

Confused, Alfred called me. After hearing him out, I, too, had bad vibes, but I suggested that he sleep on it just to be sure. But he was so eager to get someone in place that he ignored his intuition and my suggestion to sleep on it and hired the guy the same day.

Once on the job, Alfred's employee proved to be all that he promised under the assumption that he'd become a partner. Two years later, sufficiently trained to take over fully, the man unexpectedly quit, taking half the kitchen staff with him to open his own nearly identical restaurant in the same area. According to the grapevine, that was his plan all along—to learn the business at my client's expense and then go out on his own. Alfred was furious . . . but he wasn't really surprised. By not giving himself the time to reflect, he ended up having to start all over again.

Your Turn

Whether you're looking to hire, be hired, or gain new contacts, write down exactly what you want in your pocket notebook. Include not only skills, money, and schedule requirements, but also qualities of soul, personality, ethics, character, and intention. Every morning this week, read your list out loud as a way of energetically broadcasting it to the world, concentrating on what you're reading for a few minutes. By doing so, you'll telepathically connect with the perfect person or situation to fill your need and draw them into your energy field.

When interviewing or meeting with an individual, slow down, breathe deeply, and listen—not just to words, but to the energy behind the words. Listen for talents and skills to see if they match your requirements. Be relaxed and avoid feeling urgent. Don't rush your decision. Sleep on things before you make up your mind. If you aren't sure, listen to your heart over your head, and trust your vibes over your logic.

BOTTOM LINE:

Make sure "the shoe fits," then sleep on it.

STRATEGY #22

FIND YOUR SOUNDING BOARDS

You'll never learn to trust your intuition if you waste time and energy hiding it for fear that you'll be ridiculed or dismissed as a weirdo by your colleagues. It's true that there are an awful lot of five-sensory people in the business world who would laugh at you because they aren't comfortable with anyone's vibes, especially their own. Rather than abandoning yours so as not to be rejected, only to regret it later by paying a high business price, find people to whom you can tell your feelings freely and remain true to yourself.

If you're new at voicing your vibes, it's helpful to seek out role models who surround themselves with kindred spirits. My favorite six-sensory role model is Christ—after all, before he began his mission, he surrounded himself with 12 helpers.

Start searching in obvious places, such as your home: Do you have a spouse, partner, child, parent, or sibling who might be willing to listen? Might your friends or neighbors be kindred spirits? Take a look around the office as well—maybe you have a supporter at the desk next to you and you don't even realize it. For example, I once had a client who worked for a pharmaceutical company. Feeling that her co-workers were too conservative to share her spiritual and metaphysical interests, she kept her pursuits to herself. One day she took my book *Trust Your Vibes* with her to read on her break. When she took it out of her purse to fish for her lipstick, a fellow employee seized it immediately, asking what it was about. When my client explained that it was a book about intuition, her co-worker launched into an enthusiastic account of all the vibes she herself got. In three minutes they instantly bonded over the subject of vibes.

"Who knew?" my client laughingly recounted. "From looking at her I would never have guessed in a million years that these things would have interested her. Now that's all we talk about on our breaks!"

The point I'm trying to make is this: *Never assume that you can tell anything about anyone else based on appearances alone.* We're all far more complicated and interesting than we seem to be. Also, keep in mind that the more comfortable you are with your vibes, the more accepting people around you will be. If you see your vibes as weird or get defensive about them, why in the world would anyone else accept them as worthwhile? If, on the other hand, you talk matter-of-factly about your sixth sense without a lot of drama, other people will give it consideration—and even pipe up with vibes of their own.

I experienced this in a rather dramatic way shortly after the 9/11 tragedy. I was invited by a very enthusiastic special-events facilitator from a law firm in Washington, D.C., to speak to a group of 300 women who were mostly engaged in government contracts.

The coordinator said that she thought my presentation would encourage these ladies to hone their intuitive abilities in the wake of 9/11 and the anthrax scares. Yet just before she introduced me, she became afraid that the audience would think that I, and consequently she, was a weirdo. "What shall I say you do?" she asked, panicking.

"Well, we can't control what they think," I said. "And the only thing you *can* tell them is the truth. But I have a better idea: I'll introduce myself rather than have you do it. That way, we won't start with explanations as damage control."

Taking the microphone, I confidently explained my mission without hesitation or apology, speaking to the group as if I were addressing the most receptive, sympathetic audience on Earth. In my mind and heart, I was. The end result was that I got a standing ovation and was asked back to teach an extended course. Why? Because I didn't burden them with the task of validating me.

Surrounded all my life by a supportive team of family, friends, and teachers, I'm totally comfortable with my vibes and wear them like a second skin. I never could have arrived at such a state of confidence by myself. My being so at ease put the audience at ease. In addition, I wasn't looking to my audience for agreement—I was simply there to share my message and be on my way. From my observation, the people who are most successfully six-sensory, especially at work, choose a few core people to freely sound out their vibes with and then bring those insights to the table at work with a comfort level that reassures everyone.

If you share your intuition on the job and get a strong negative reaction, it's imperative that you *do not* get defensive. Just say something like, "I can see how you'd think that. Sometimes even I wonder if my vibes are plain crazy—yet they usually turn out to make sense in the long run, at least for me. It's okay if you don't agree. I'm fine with that."

Don't set yourself up for unnecessary conflict, rejection, or ridicule at work by posturing that your vibes are "right." Just insist that they feel right *for you* and you're willing to stand by them, at least for now. The point is to suggest rather that your vibes are your own, and that you trust them enough to say so and act on them, even if it's uncomfortable to do so.

Whether or not you choose to share your vibes at work is up to you. Use your judgment. If you give it a try, take a playful approach rather than a defensive posture. Just don't feel that you have to wing it alone.

Your Turn

This week, make a list in your pocket notebook of all the positive role models you can think of, both familiar and distant. Describe who they are and what they do that inspires you. Using your list for motivation, concentrate your vibes on attracting kindred spirits, influential role models, and safe sounding boards to your life. If you can already identify such people, connect with them at least twice this week to share your vibes. The more you connect with kindred spirits, the more comfortable you'll become with expressing your intuition and staying faithful to what feels true for now.

THE BOTTOM LINE:

Seek safe sounding boards and positive role models.

STRATEGY #23

BROADCAST GOOD VIBES

When it comes to using your intuition, you'll soon realize that it's practical for far more than just tuning in to information to guide you on the job—it also transmits a subtle beacon of communication to the world at large and attracts exactly what you seek. By trusting your vibes, this "two-way radio" creates an immediate magnetic vibration that sets into motion what most people call "synchronicity," or the ability to be in just the right place at the right time.

Awakening your sixth sense and putting it to proper use eliminates the need to worry about finding the right job or opportunity because it draws those things directly to you. The best part is that doing so communicates the vibration from your Higher Self and not merely your emotionally based conscious mind; consequently, it attracts a far better and more satisfying outcome than your ego mind could ever imagine.

My client Denise, for instance, was very frustrated in her job as a sales representative for a large Midwestern pharmaceutical company, as she'd fantasized for years about working in the television and film industry. She never took steps in the direction she loved for fear that she didn't have the necessary skills . . . or a chance. Instead, she spent the time calling on clients feeling resentful and bored.

When Denise came to me, I asked her to suspend her beliefs and assumptions about the job she really wanted and not even try to get into her dream job directly. Instead, I advised her to use sixth sense to attract an *opportunity.*

Confused and thinking I was crazy, Denise said that she couldn't conceive of how to do that. I suggested that she use each chance she got to tell any- and everyone including herself, how much she'd love to work in film and TV. Rather than hide her love, as most five-sensory people do, I told her to announce it, at full volume and with great enthusiasm, and watch what happened.

You see, the sixth sense is centered in the heart and powerfully communicates to others what you love and hold dearest. Most five-sensory people shut down their hearts (and their sixth sense) and instead of "I love," frequently broadcast "I hate": "I hate my job, I hate my office, I hate my boss, I hate the people I work with, I hate my long hours," and so forth. If you pay attention, you'll be astonished by how often you hear it from others—and from yourself.

These words set up an intense and repelling vibration, pushing people and opportunities as far away from you as possible. But by sending out the vibration of what you love, you'll immediately create a dynamic, magnetic, and attractive vibration that literally pulls people and opportunities related to your love to you. After all, six-sensories know that there's no magic involved in life; there are only the dynamic laws of attraction at work.

Although she was dubious, Denise gave broadcasting her love a try. The first thing she noticed is that the job she thought she hated got easier—and the conversations she had with her customers took a very interesting turn.

Cautious at first, and not wanting to appear unprofessional, Denise began to strike up conversations with her clients about how she'd love to get a foot in movies or TV. Six months later, a supplier that she'd always had a positive rapport with called to ask if she'd be interested in doing some sales-training videos for his company. He said that the company wanted to market several new products, and they'd decided that a training video was the most cost-effective way to reach all the reps. He told Denise that they were going to hire a professional actress, but since she was so interested in film, he was offering her the opportunity because her experience would make her more persuasive.

Feeling shy, my client almost said no—but following her vibes, she agreed. Not only was she a natural on camera, but she also helped write, direct, and star in the video. And with her success, she was hired to make more marketing videos. By broadcasting her love, Denise attracted opportunities that she didn't even know existed.

I often run into people just like Denise—those who have no idea what they want to do or how to begin looking for a job they'd love, so they're stuck in work that carries no spark. If this is the case with you, first look at your present broadcast and how often you say "I hate." Even in casual conversation, these two little words are potent saboteurs that set up a repugnant, dissonant vibration that distances you from others and shuts all doors of opportunity.

Next, change your mental tuner from *What's wrong with this picture?* to *What's right?* and begin to consciously broadcast what you love. Never mind being a "professional" and keeping your desires to yourself—all human beings respond positively to enthusiastic communication. Have you ever heard the saying "All the world loves a lover"? Well, it's true. No matter what your job entails, being upbeat and loving in your communication will improve it.

Now, if you're afraid to share yourself in your present job because your heart isn't in it, that's understandable. But do share it with everyone else outside the job as often as you can. What I'm suggesting is networking, but with a twist: Take your networking to a higher, more spiritual level of love.

I'm reminded of Bob, who was the best UPS delivery man ever. Every time he showed up at my door he had a smile, a joke, and a minute to ask how I was. But the truth was that Bob didn't like his job. He was overweight and had a heart condition, and the physical demands and hours were way too long and hard on him. His job didn't allow him time with his four kids, all of whom were under the age of ten. What Bob *did* love—and talked about often—was the idea of opening a small postal mart where he could ship packages, rent mailboxes, and provide modest office services without running all over town. He didn't have the money, but he talked incessantly about what he'd love to do should his ship come in.

One day a new delivery guy showed up. When I asked about Bob, he said that UPS just bought out the postal-mart business and set Bob up in a shop of his own near his house. Apparently, what he loved was heard and came to him.

THE FIVE-SENSORY WORLD IS QUICK TO dismiss laws of attraction as nonsense, saying that it's better to just "pound the pavement." Well, before you dismiss the notion of positive broadcasting, do some research of your own and ask ten people who you know really love their work how they got their jobs. I'm certain that at least eight will say that broadcasting their love attracted their opportunity in some way. Now this doesn't mean that you don't have to take conventional steps to secure a job as well. Of course, you must do all it takes to get where you're going, including learning the necessary skills. But if you'd truly love the job you aspire to, you've either already learned some of the skills, or you'd be willing to do whatever it takes to acquire them.

What I'm suggesting here does not in any way advise you to neglect other doors to opportunity, but rather to open all of them. By all means, knock on every door possible when seeking what you want in your work. But be aware that we're all energetically connected to one another in a great vibrational matrix that seeks harmony, resonance, and balance. By broadcasting your heart, you'll be sending a signal throughout this matrix, which in turn will attract what your heart seeks.

This works not only when looking for new job opportunities, but also when seeking clients, locations, investors, and even employees. The key is to not only broadcast what you love, but to follow what you broadcast.

My client Tamara desperately wanted to work for Oprah Winfrey's company, Harpo, here in Chicago, even though she had no particular skills or talents to get a job there. When I asked her what she loved, she laughingly said, "At the moment, three things: people, Oprah, and Starbucks chai lattes." I told her to broadcast her love of people and Oprah and enjoy her chai lattes at the same time.

Every morning on her way to work as a substitute teacher for the Chicago public-school system, Tamara would stop at Starbucks for her chai latte. While waiting in line, she'd talk to others who were waiting about her loves, especially Oprah and her heart's desire to work for the media queen. Two months later, a fellow in line told Tamara that his sister worked for Oprah, and she'd mentioned that they were hiring several interns for the upcoming season. He gave her his sister's phone number and wished her luck. With her chai latte in hand, Tamara called the man's sister and recounted her story. Her enthusiastic sharing got her an interview.

My point is that you never know whom you're talking to and what their ability to support your heart might be. Expect the best when you communicate, because the Universe is helping you behind the scenes.

Another client, Miriam, worked as an administrative nurse at Cook County Hospital and was burned-out by her taxing job. All she wanted to do was move to Hawaii and work with flowers or gardens. She kept telling me, "In my next life, I'll be in Maui instead of in hell, which is where I work now."

I encouraged her to broadcast what she loved, and follow it up by taking a flower-arranging class after work and on weekends. Claiming to be too tired, she declined, but I challenged this as an excuse. "If you love it, it will give you energy, not take it."

Miriam finally followed her vibes and enrolled in a one-week flower-arranging course while on vacation. Not surprisingly, she loved the class and enrolled in every flower-arranging course she could find once she got home—and she soon mastered the art. While in class she talked endlessly about Hawaii and her dream. A few months later, a classmate who worked for an international hotel chain told her that there was a job opening at the flower shop in one of their hotels near the Honolulu airport.

Miriam seized the opportunity and got the job. Within a year her skill was recognized throughout the hotel chain. Two years later she was invited to fill the position at one of the chain's hotels in Maui. She didn't even have to ask for her dream job—it asked for her.

Six-sensories know that by broadcasting and following your vibes, they will draw you directly to what you love. For every step you take following your heart, the Universe takes a step toward you.

Your Turn

Every day this week, write down ten things in your pocket notebook that you love in life and why. It can be as superficial as a fresh cup of mocha java or as deep as your children. Then during the day, speak freely of what you love to any safe person who will listen. Be enthusiastic and generous in your sharing—open your heart and reveal what you care about and enjoy most in life. And have fun as you do this! Watch how your vibes shift when your attention focuses on what you love, and how those around you change and open up to you as well.

Pay close attention to your words, both written and spoken, carefully editing out the words, thoughts, and vibration of *I hate*. If you find yourself saying "I hate," take a breath and say, "Enough of that. This is what I love." Before getting out of bed in the morning, verbalize ten things you love, and follow at least one that day. Before going to bed at night, name out loud ten things you loved doing that day.

Broadcast what you love to let people know that you're

ready, willing, and able to serve that cause. Be open, and expect your broadcast to fall on receptive ears. Make a game of sending out love, and have fun with it: "I love calls from people with great opportunities," "I love calling on clients," "I love being an entrepreneur and starting my own business," or even "I love myself." Then expect your heart's desire to show up. Good business relationships are, at their core, good relationships, period. And the best relationships are based on love.

THE BOTTOM LINE:

Broadcast what you love and you'll attract your heart's desire.

STRATEGY #24

REMEMBER THAT YOU GET WHAT YOU GIVE

One of the unwavering laws of the universe is that you get what you give, plain and simple. The returns you're experiencing today directly reflect the effort you've put into realizing your goals. In other words, just getting into the flow of what you love isn't going to be enough to succeed. Like a train sitting on the tracks, you still must use your creative engine to get your business moving.

Invariably, when I encounter a truly successful person, the first thing I notice is the determined commitment and relentless effort that person has put into his or her dreams. I've never seen an accidental success, but I *have* witnessed serendipitous ones. It may seem to the naïve, untrained eye that it was all luck, but if you look again, you'll see consistency and commitment, coupled with the intention to create and improve what's already there. Altogether, this creates some of the most powerful and magnetic vibrations there are. Halfway measures, sloppy efforts, and unfaithful attention, on the other hand, only create frustration and disappointment.

This makes me think of Kendra, a client who loved acting and whose intuition told her it was her true calling. Yet she did nothing about it until she came to one of my workshops about trusting your vibes. Remembering her passion and wanting to give it a chance, she signed up for a basic acting course. Then she got her head shots and dove back in the arena.

Two months later, Kendra arrived at my door, disappointed and annoyed that her career on Broadway hadn't materialized. "My vibes—and you—misled me!" she cried. "I haven't gotten a single job yet!"

Tickled at her unrealistic expectations, especially given her shallow efforts, I laughed out loud. "You're on track," I said, "but no one else is going to drive your train. You may love acting, but your efforts aren't enough to demand the returns you ask. So stop pointing your finger at me and look at the other four pointing back at you. In other words, quit complaining and go to work—if you want it that much, do whatever it takes to succeed."

Shocked that I'd thrown her bad attitude right back at her, it was Kendra's turn to laugh. "I'm being unrealistic, aren't I?" she admitted. "I guess I'm just not committed enough."

Apparently she rethought her approach and stuck with it, because 15 years later she landed a wonderful role on a TV series. I was happy for her—she'd realized her dream after all.

KEEP IN MIND THAT FAIRY TALES (and television) give us the impression that success comes immediately after we realize what we really want, like an instant reward for being honest and taking a risk. While there *is* such a reward, I've never seen an instant one. It only comes after combining your interest with years of dedication, refining and perfecting your skills until you master them. Intuitively we all know that there's no such thing as a free lunch—each of us gets what we give.

Unfortunately, most five-sensory people don't want to commit to the kind of focused work and dedication it takes to succeed in what they love. They'd rather show up at work, do the minimum, and complain that no one's taking better care of them. They spend their time mooning over their disappointments instead of doing what my teachers taught me was the only direct way to success: *Suit up, shut up, show up, and do your work. The rest will take care of itself.*

The more you give of your love to your job, the more it will give back to you—I guarantee it. This is the only way to the top, because the top isn't a leap you make, but a ladder you climb . . . slowly but surely. If you're stuck and uninspired at work, continue what you're doing right now with heartfelt, consistent commitment, and see what happens. What genuine effort are you making to improve and refine your ability? What attention are you giving to doing the best job you possibly can? Assuming that you're not suffering in a job you dislike, what emotional and creative investments are you making?

I spoke to a young man recently who was really frustrated in his sales position. He was far below his quota, afraid that he'd lose his territory if his record didn't improve, and worried that he'd looked bad to his boss at the quarterly sales meeting. "Man, I try," he assured me, "but it's so hard out there."

Although he talked a good game, his vibration didn't resonate with what he was saying. He was trying all right . . . to avoid doing his job. He consistently reported to work five minutes late; and he chatted with the secretaries, checked his e-mail, and surfed the Web before making a single sales call. He spent 50 percent of his day schmoozing people other than clients. He knew it (so did I), and his results bore out the facts. This guy's vibration was scattered; his prospects, sensing this, didn't feel confident placing their orders with him. So they didn't.

He laughed when I pointed out how incongruent his vibration was with his stated goals and how obvious it was to his clients that he wasn't committed to doing a good job. I told him that if he asked people to invest their confidence and money in him, then he'd better be in a position (energetically) to match their investment with his own.

Remember the following: Not only do you get what you give from the universe, you get it from your clients, co-workers, and employees as well. The law of mutuality is "Energy out, energy in." And this governs *all* relationships. So, in order to elevate your vibration and realize your business objectives, be consistent, committed, and reliable. Do your part, and the Universe will meet you halfway.

Your Turn

Six-sensory people are fully aware of the magnetic power of consistent, committed intention to create. Next to love, nothing is more compelling. A man on a mission attracts an army—the wandering man gets lost and ignored.

Experiment with focused intention at work this week and watch what happens. Start every day by writing your intentions down in your notebook. Keep it simple—a sentence or two for each goal at the most. Then, before you go home each evening, write down what happened that concerned your goals. Observe what you attract from your co-workers and your boss. And be prepared for positive surprises.

Also, take steps this week to improve upon something you already love to do. Take a class, attend a lecture, or at the very minimum, read a motivational book. Record your activities and your experiences in your pocket notebook. Did you meet any potential new friends? Did you encounter anyone you might work with in the future? Did you have a good time? Did you get any new inspiration?

When you're at work, be creative and approach your job as if it were a work of art. How can you make it more elegant or beautiful? If you want something more, *give* something more: Stay overtime if you must, seek a mentor, work harder, and stick with it. In your pocket notebook, record the times when you went the extra mile this week and what happened as a result. Take what you get and create something better.

THE BOTTOM LINE:

Give it your all.

STRATEGY #25

EMPLOY BAD-VIBE BUSTERS

One of the greatest challenges people in the workplace face is staving off bad vibes. Nothing can turn an enthusiastic mood around more quickly or throw a wet blanket on the creative fires on the job than a solid dose of downer energy from someone you work with. In fact, it should be viewed as the number one work hazard to avoid at all costs.

Just as toxic as radiation poisoning, negative energy is disastrous to human beings. Don't be misled into thinking that because bad vibes are invisible or hard to identify at their source that they're any less deadly to your creative genius than poisonous gas—they aren't. And don't be conned into believing that denying or ignoring negativity will protect you from its deadly effects either—it won't.

Bad vibes weigh you down, irritate your nervous system, depress your mood, leave you doubting your self-worth, distract you, and make you defensive. And if you must ward off all that craziness, then needless to say there will be little energy left over to actually do your job, let alone do it well.

The other day I walked past the TV as it was airing the five o'clock news. Seeing dozens of people from a local government office being taken out on stretchers by emergency workers, I anxiously asked my husband what had happened. Jokingly, he said, "The boss was in a bad mood and gave everyone a psychic attack. It took out the entire department."

"Well, finally people are telling the truth," I said, "and getting the care they need after such an assault." Although his crack was funny, I still shook my head.

Jokes or not, "psychic attacks" (my personal expression for the effects of being derailed by negative or bad vibes) are real and debilitating. And they're the main reason people quit their jobs, more so even than not making enough money. The good news is that you can protect yourself against negativity in the workplace. The even better news is if you're really creative, you can actually do something to stop it.

First, identify the problem. The most challenging thing about negativity at work is that it feels politically dangerous to acknowledge that it even exists, let alone point it out. Like the elephant in the middle of the room that everyone pretends isn't there, the person spreading bad vibes is rarely confronted by others for fear of being accused of harassment.

But denial is no protection, and neither is pretending that you don't feel anything. Although it's a noble effort, denying or ignoring negativity in the workplace is not a sound strategy for protection—after all, the bomb will still tick, taking everyone down by the minute. Until you acknowledge that there is, in fact, a problem, you can't solve it. As Carl Jung once said, when the diagnosis is correct, the healing begins. So honestly see any case of bad vibes for what they are, because until then, you won't be able to dismantle them.

8 WAYS TO HANDLE BAD VIBES ON THE JOB

1. Start by recognizing the quality of the energetic atmosphere at work every day. Run a "vibe check" before you take your place: Good vibes feel calm, clear, relaxed, and happy; while bad vibes feel dark, tense, brittle, and even dangerous. Simply testing the psychic temperature of the workplace will allow you to make the necessary adjustments to keep your own energy intact.

2. If you do a vibe check and all is clear, take a deep breath and enter with an open heart. However, if you sense some dissonance, take another deep breath, get grounded, surround yourself with positive vibes, and resolve that you won't let anything you encounter throw you off center.

3. As you enter dubious territory, don't take any negativity you run into personally. Just resolve to let it bounce off you, and commit to focusing only on your goals and intentions for the day. Doing this will protect you from unfavorable distractions more than anything else.

4. Once you diagnose bad vibes, outwardly acknowledge them in some way, if only to yourself—but (and this is extremely important) be discreet and subtle. You don't need to announce them to the entire office, and I don't recommend doing so. That will only aggravate the problem and spread the negativity you want to clear even more.

5. Next, be kind, loving, and patient with those around you, especially the bad-vibe dispensers (BVD for short), because they need it. Focus on work, and if negative conversation arises, listen neutrally and compassionately if you can't gracefully get away. However, be sure that you don't get involved with or rescue anyone.

8 WAYS TO HANDLE BAD VIBES ON THE JOB, *cont'd.*

6. Observe, don't absorb, what's going on around you. If you can unobtrusively escape, do so. Your left foot and right foot are two of your most powerful defenses against negativity in the workplace: Turn them in the opposite direction of the problem and leave.

7. If you can't remain neutral or make a run for it, surrender and accept the situation. Give the identified BVD your complete attention for five full minutes. Encourage him or her to complain, gossip, attack, whine, or whatever modus operandi is being used to his or her heart's content.

8. In the meantime, just listen, breathe, and stay neutral—don't engage, resonate, or rescue. When the five minutes have passed, ask with complete sincerity if there's anything you can personally do to help right now. Emphasize the *right now* part. If you hear, "Yes, there is," and you *can* help, then I suggest you do so. If you hear, "No, not really," then say, "I'm sorry. I really hope it works out." Then go back to work.

If your BVD refuses to answer your question, ask again, and repeat the question until he or she can no longer ignore it. Then either help or go back to work. Stick to this plan no matter who the BVD is. It works.

ARE *YOU* A BVD?

Now before you start projecting your BVD suspicions onto anyone else at work, do a little self-examining to see if you're the office BVD. Classic causes of bad-vibe behavior are:

- being hungry, angry, or tired;
- being lonely or depressed;
- suffering from PMS, indigestion, or a headache;
- being overwhelmed or unclear on your tasks; or
- avoiding your own job and using commotion and drama to cover it up.

In other words, be honest. Before you point the "bad-vibes finger" at anyone else, remember that four more are pointing at you. If you're guilty of any of the aforementioned BVD behaviors, chances are that the negativity of others means they're just fighting back. Rather than denying your mood and condition, be an adult and take responsibility for what you bring to the job. Acknowledge that as human beings we affect one another energetically. Never mind hiding behind your "professional" demeanor or your position—if you're in a funk, a phony smile or a fancy title won't cover it up. Just be real and take responsibility for what you put out.

Sometimes simply admitting that you're feeling negative begins to dispel it. Just announce, "Forgive me, but I'm in a bad mood right now. It has nothing to do with you." Then set your attitude aside and get on with the day. This is far more considerate than spreading your negativity like a virus, only to have it boomerang back and flatten you by the end of the day. And believe me, it will.

Taking responsibility for the energy you bring to the workplace is the most proactive step you can take in assuring good vibes at work. Sleep enough, eat breakfast, turn on classical music rather than the morning news if you must listen to something, and leave home early enough to arrive at the office on time. Pay attention to what causes your drama, and then slowly and surely move away from it.

As I mentioned before, sometimes all it takes to change or release negative energy is to acknowledge that it's there. You don't have to announce it to the world, just to yourself and to anyone it's affecting. The important thing to remember is how powerful you and your energy are. Whether you're the mail runner or the boss, you affect people more than you realize (or want to admit), especially if you bring a less-than-positive vibe to the place.

Money covers a multitude of sins, but not all of them. Take, for example, my client Abigail. An insurance broker who ran a ten-person firm for more than 20 years, Abigail paid her staff well, gave them bonuses, kept the workdays short, and except for three weeks during the fall home-buying season, rarely asked for overtime. She thought that she was a great boss and felt that her staff should love her because she was so fair and generous.

What my client didn't acknowledge was that she was also a seriously negative person. She was irritable, curt, impatient, disrespectful, and even rude to her employees. She was a poor listener because she was consumed with her own drama and didn't pay attention to anything they tried to tell her. With four teenagers at home, a struggling marriage, and some poor investments haunting her, Abigail carried her anxiety everywhere and infected everyone with it.

When she went on a business trip to Europe, seven members of her staff—including two of her best salespeople—quit without notice, leaving her high and dry. How could these individuals whom she'd treated so well do such a dastardly deed? Their reason was simply that Abigail had spread too many bad vibes for too long, and they'd had it. So, humbled and nearly bankrupt, my client finally got the point and cleaned up her energetic act in a hurry.

In business, more than any other arena, I think it's important to realize that despite our professional exteriors, we're in fact highly sensitive, emotional, responsive beings who react to far more than we acknowledge. We're living, breathing, sensitive, psychic entities who are naturally pulled toward what feels good and away from what doesn't. The more positive people feel in our presence, the more time, energy, creativity, and money they'll invest in us.

So it makes good business sense to be the bearer of good vibes. That means that you need to show up to work with good intentions *and* energy. If you have a bad day, admit it and move on. If it happens regularly, admit that you have a problem and deal with it on your own time outside of work. It's not fair to your co-workers, and it will ultimately hurt you and your paycheck.

Finally, don't gossip, since this brings around serious bad vibes. Breathe through any malicious chat you may encounter and don't respond—just keep breathing. Gossip is so toxic that you shouldn't touch it with a ten-foot pole. Not only is such talk itself negative, but engaging in it throws you into a telepathic loop that keeps you feeling unsafe and in danger no matter where you are. Let gossip burn itself out by nonparticipation: It will pass, and the negativity won't stick to you.

Your Turn

This week, become the bearer of good news—and good vibes—at work. Start by appreciating those you work with by giving out sincere compliments and acknowledging their efforts. Ask about your colleagues' families, their vacations, their work challenges, and even their pets. Just let them know that you care about them and want to spread a little light into their day. Be encouraging and support them. Share a joke or a positive bit of news instead of being the office "downer." Laugh and smile, even if you don't feel like it.

In your notebook, jot down the compliments you gave and to whom all week, and their results. View your efforts as planting an energetic garden of good vibes—soon you'll reap a wonderful return!

THE BOTTOM LINE:

Be positive.

STRATEGY #26

CLAIM YOUR SPACE

It happens to the best of us: No one is immune, regardless of their position. Usually it occurs when we least expect it, when we're happily minding our own business and fully enjoying our job. I'm talking about the person who drives us crazy.

It might be a boss, an employee, a co-worker, or even a client—no matter who it is, this person has the ability to get on our last nerve, to make us want to scream and pull our hair out and then make a mad dash for the exit.

Often the person we can't stand sneaks up on us and catches us off guard. He or she may be friendly at first, or at least pretend to be. It soon becomes apparent, however, that he or she is dangerous to our mental health and clearly doesn't value us or the work.

A particular type of bad-vibe dispenser (BVD), this type of person operates in a number of offensive ways: Whether it's interrupting us when we're speaking, ignoring what we're saying, trespassing on our turf, not doing what we ask, or simply breathing the wrong way, everything about them disturbs our tranquility, incites our anger, and makes us question our abilities.

While these people may feel like our worst nightmare, we six-sensories know that, in fact, they're in our life to serve as teachers on a spiritual level. Their effect on us is only as negative as is our need to get to a deeper place of self-awareness. Learning to effectively deal with people like this without losing our cool or letting our vibrations be disturbed is a victory that will serve us for life. So when we run into someone we can't stand on the job, we six-sensories know that we're being welcomed to the classroom of personal boundaries. It's time for us to grow.

The first lesson is to take nothing these annoying people say or do personally. Nothing about their offensive behavior has one iota to do with you—thinking otherwise puts you at their mercy. They're usually so self-absorbed that they'll be quite insensitive to anything going on around them, including you. The minute you feel offended by their behavior, you'll abandon your own center of gravity and fuse your vibration with theirs. The best way to keep from being thrown off balance is to remain detached, which lets you see these people coming, and allows you to energetically take cover.

To keep your cool, learn to breathe correctly under fire—in through your nose and out through your mouth, gently releasing the sound "Aah" as you do. The longer you must interact with the negative force, the more often you should do this.

Another useful technique is to periodically and silently do an objective reality check that will help you keep your center of gravity: "That's the window. This is my telephone. She's the office troublemaker. This is the copier." All the while, breathe and say, "Aah." And if you still find yourself becoming agitated, physically move away. This will break their energy field and disconnect you from their vibes. When you move, you help stay in your own skin and out of theirs.

Another way to protect yourself is to mentally define your boundaries so that the other person's vibration can't seep into yours through holes of weakness. Rather than considering Mr. or Ms. Negative as the problem, recognize that the real problem is a weakness in *your* energy field that needs to be corrected. The greater the aggravation you feel, the more you're being put on notice to strengthen your boundaries. Having strong limits gives you the ability to say no and let everyone know what you're comfortable with. If you don't communicate your limits, how can you expect an insensitive boor to know them? It's your job, not theirs, to make your boundaries clear.

When you feel ready to scream at someone's behavior, step back, breathe, and see exactly what they're doing that crosses the line. And be as specific as possible. For example, I once had a secretary who had the habit of laughing like a foghorn throughout the day. I let her go on like this until one day I got so fed up that I thought I was going to wrestle her to the ground and silence her by stuffing a sock in her mouth. I stepped back instead, breathed deeply for several moments, and observed exactly what was going on. I discovered that she was either logged on to a jokes Website or schmoozing with friends rather than doing her job.

Having diagnosed the problem, I then had to address the solution, which was the tricky part. I had to confront her and say, "No, this is out of bounds and must stop now." The key to successfully doing this is twofold: (1) You must deliver the message in an even-toned, unemotional way and mean it; and (2) you must be willing to be the bad guy.

The people who get aggravated the most at work are usually the ones who are the nicest, or the office wimps. I know because I was one of them. Rather than sounding mean or unkind, I allowed myself to be stomped on repeatedly. (Of course, this kind of behavior doesn't work—not only do you lose self-respect, you lose *everyone's* respect. The way to get past this and energetically strengthen your boundaries is to redefine the word *no* in your mind. Rather than thinking of no as a negative, think of it as a positive, or better yet, a creative directive.)

Finally deciding that I was willing to be unpopular, I took several deep breaths, walked around the office, calmed my heart, and quietly said to my secretary, "Even though I can see that you're enjoying yourself laughing about non-work-related matters, it's distracting and prevents us both from doing our jobs. Please stop, and focus on what you're here to do. I'd appreciate your cooperation." It was difficult, but she stopped, and I lived through it.

I had to do the same thing three more times, and each time it got easier. A week later, the woman quit—her service to me was complete. Once I learned my lesson, we energetically went our separate ways. That's how it works.

STUDYING BOUNDARIES IN DEPTH, I've learned that they're best sustained when a particular area is balanced and energized: what in the metaphysical world is called the "third chakra," and in professional jargon I call your "power center." Located two inches below your navel, this place represents the very center of your being. It's the balancing point in your body where information and experiences are taken in and processed, and then responses are executed.

The stronger this psychic center of gravity is, the more powerful your ability to remain in charge and deal with things appropriately (instead of lose control and react poorly) will be. Consider your power center the throne upon which your consciousness rests, guarding and guiding the kingdom called your life.

One of the most important faculties for your power center to control is your emotions, and the way to do that is to breathe. Practice deep breathing whenever your boundaries are strained or tested, so you can remain detached and unemotional as you decide how to respond. Imagine as you breathe that your power center is a brilliant, golden disk of sovereign clarity where you can place any disturbance and dissolve it. By calmly and consistently breathing, you'll be able to take control over your problems, put them in the proper perspective, and make productive decisions about them.

8 WAYS TO ESTABLISH YOUR BOUNDARIES AT WORK

1. Whenever any challenge or disturbance to your psychic equilibrium or vibration arises, activate your power by breathing in though your nose and out through your mouth, and saying, "Aah."

2. Continue to do this for several seconds. As you breathe, you'll calm down.

3. Next, mentally place the disturbing energetic element (your irritable assistant, your competitive co-worker, the client who just cancelled his order, or what have you) in your power center, which is located just below your belly button, and continue to breathe.

4. As you observe the person in your power center, imagine neutralizing his or her negative effect on you with each breath.

8 WAYS TO ESTABLISH YOUR BOUNDARIES AT WORK, *cont'd.*

5. If you feel excessively charged about the person or situation, increase the volume of your "Aah" to a stronger "Ha!" as though expelling something from your throat or chest, and indeed from your energy field.

6. You can thump your chest and belly for more impact, as though performing a subtle Heimlich maneuver on yourself. There's no need to be unduly loud when you expel your "Ha!"—you can even do it under your breath if necessary, and it will still work.

7. If you attract unwanted attention as you clear your energy field of draining or irritating energy, simply tell your onlooker that you're sighing and getting a hit of oxygen. You may get a raised eyebrow or two, but usually this works to get the offending person to back off.

8. After several rounds of this, the person who challenges your boundaries may very well leave you alone for good. Try it—it works.

Practice this kind of mindful breathing whenever you find yourself becoming unglued or overwhelmed by another's intensity. Doing so on a regular basis keeps you grounded and calm, and helps you maintain your serenity and ability to objectively assess the agendas of those you work with so you can make powerful grounded decisions for yourself. The benefit to doing this is that you come to know, respect, and defend your limits. And the surprising outcome is that when you respect your boundaries, so does everyone else.

To sum up, six-sensory people recognize every situation as an opportunity to grow. If you're challenged by someone who makes you crazy, see this person as your temporary teacher—your lesson is to strengthen your boundaries. Learn the lesson, and the teacher will be on his or her way.

Your Turn

This week, write down every time someone gets under your skin and notice exactly what they're doing. Then decide to dismantle their negative effect on you immediately by stepping into your power center. Do this by gently breathing in through your nose and out through your mouth several times (or until you begin to feel calm). Imagine a brilliant golden disc rotating in front of your belly button as you breathe, blocking all negativity from coming into your body and influencing your mood or peace of mind. Next, mentally envision that your workplace is your personal kingdom. Using your imagination, walk though your realm as though you're in absolute command and control.

As you encounter the aggravating person in your kingdom, check in with yourself to see if you're taking the irritation personally, and if so, emotionally step back and stop it. As you do, ask yourself if you're willing to be unpopular by claiming your boundaries and enforcing them by offering a solid and direct no to the offending person. If you are, find your courage, take a deep breath, and then calmly and clearly communicate that no to the offensive person while remaining friendly. That should take care of the problem.

THE BOTTOM LINE:

Strengthen your boundaries.

STRATEGY #27

UNDERSTAND THE POWER OF DOING NOTHING

Have you ever stopped to think about where you are and what you're doing when you get your best ideas and greatest intuitive flashes? When I ask my clients, most of them realize that it's when they're enjoying a walk in nature, are just waking up on a lazy Sunday morning, are driving in the silence of a solo car trip, or are taking a snooze on a long airplane journey. Rarely do I hear someone say that their brightest ideas come while they're rushing through a hectic workday.

Although we may accomplish the business at hand during a day's work, we're mostly using our logical, linear left brain as we do so. Intuitive flashes, however, don't come through this conscious channel of the brain—instead, our creative insights come through the right brain, a channel we access best when we're relaxing, daydreaming, and experiencing a moment of quiet time.

As you race through your days, you take in a lot that you just don't notice. All of this information isn't lost—it's simply stored for you to access at a later, quieter time (that is, if you ever give yourself that time). To tune in to your vibes, you must shift your focus away from external activity. In other words, stop the onslaught of information—whether it's from your computer, your cell phone, your co-workers, your boss, your employees, or anything else that demands your attention—then go within yourself and simply take in what's there.

When I was a student early in the process of developing my intuition, my teachers often suggested that sometimes the most direct way to access my sixth sense was to do absolutely nothing . . . or at least nothing intense or concentrated in any way. Time and again, when I've needed inspiration in my professional life and it just wasn't there, if I've just backed off and left some space in my day to sit and do nothing, it always comes flying through.

I tend to do a lot in the fall, winter, and spring. The minute summer comes, however, I put the CLOSED sign up in my office and take a lazy three-week vacation with my husband and two daughters. I sleep in, hang out, go for walks, read romance novels, and stroll through shops and markets. Above all, I don't think of my work (which isn't easy because I love it so much). I cut off all communication and often go to places where there are no phones. And I don't even turn on my cell phone.

Upon return to my office, within days I'm so filled with inspiration that I invent another workshop or write another book—and it's happened for me ten years in a row. The best part in all this is that after a good rest from work, the ideas flow easily into my brain, and it's not a struggle at all. Judging from what emerges, I can see that much of my intuitive inspiration has come from all that I've experienced during the work months but have had no time to process. I just need space and time to tap in to these precious insights and take advantage of them.

Space and time have also helped the following individuals in their creative pursuits:

— My sister Cuky got her idea to start a massage-training course for families and nonprofessionals while painting her toenails on the beach. She followed through and is now traveling around the world teaching these healing techniques and having the time of her life. And she makes good money to boot.

— My brother-in-law Gene got his idea to work outside the family printing business and do metal sculpting during the quiet hours after midnight when everyone was asleep. In his first show, he sold more than half of his pieces.

— And finally, Conrad Hilton, the great hotelier, used to sit quietly in his office with the curtains drawn for hours until inspiration and insight came through.

One of the challenges many of my more successful clients face is the ability to stop working at the end of the day and just go home and relax. Fearful that if they stop, so will their enterprise, they take their work home, rarely allowing themselves to let go, unplug, and renew. Believing that this is a smart way to do business, they don't see themselves becoming drained and draining others. The worst offenders vehemently argue that they aren't doing this because they want to, but because they must.

I believe, however, that they become workaholics because they're control freaks who work from fear and infect themselves and others with a constant state of emergency. Being overly dutiful, vigilant, and controlling is rarely effective and offers little financial benefit either. For one thing, the medical and therapeutic cost of treating stress offsets any profits this slavish mentality offers.

To access your vibes and improve your finances, not to mention your health, family relationships, and love life, don't be a control freak or a workaholic. If you're a compulsive overworker, see it as an addiction and treat it accordingly. Rather than being a *work*horse who drags your job with you everywhere, become a *race*horse and run the daily track of your job. That is, do the best you can during the day—but then quit, go home, and relax and pamper yourself. It will give you the psychic juice for tomorrow's round.

The most important thing to know is that leaving the job at the end of the day doesn't necessarily mean packing up your creativity—it just shifts you from an external focus to an internal one. The minute you free your energy from what's out there, you tune in to the energy within, where bits of unconscious data and creative genius are waiting to be tapped and utilized.

One of my clients, a dedicated Realtor with only moderate success, took this advice and started a Scrabble club after work as a way to wean himself from working 24/7. While placing the word *vintage* on the board, he had a sudden inspiration to start a side business buying and selling vintage cars. Many of his real-estate clients were elderly people who were downsizing, and quite a few had great old vehicles to sell. Over the next few years, he not only built up this business, but he created a vintage-car calendar as well. Today, he has two successful businesses with six employees. But the best thing is that he's enjoying the most prosperous time of his life doing something he loves—all born from a game of Scrabble.

When interviewed, CEOs regularly say that their greatest ideas didn't come in the meeting room, but rather during their off-time, such as during vacations, relaxing drives or games of golf, or playing with their kids. So if you want to be truly proactive in using your sixth sense and tap in to your inner genius and mine creative gold, back off work at the day's end. Go home, kick back, have some fun, take some quiet time, even learn to meditate—whatever you do, make sure that you give your inner self an opportunity to incubate. Don't make the mistake of believing that just because you're not actively running the show, the show stops. Behind the scenes, all your intuitive wheels are turning at their optimal level, working to serve you.

Your Turn

See it as smart business to leave the work at the office and refresh and relax yourself at the end of the day. If you're the boss, do it for yourself—and encourage your employees to do the same. If you're an employee managed by a boss who operates in a chronic state of emergency, protect yourself from getting infected by his or her overly intense vibes by breathing easy throughout the day. Above all, don't be scared or fooled by all the drama that overdoing creates. Do your best at work, and then leave it at work. In your pocket notebook, write "I quit for the day" just before leaving . . . and then do so.

If projects do demand overtime (and they will), give it your all—but take your well-deserved break afterward. It will ensure that your creativity and intuition on the job keep flowing. Also, make it point to take mini-breaks during the day, such as a leisurely ten-minute walk instead of a hurried cup of coffee or a competitive computer game. At lunch, close your eyes and listen to baroque music instead of checking your e-mail.

The most powerful moments in music are often the spaces between the notes. I believe that the most powerful moments in business come from the rest periods as well. By taking them often, you'll allow your inner genius to come through.

THE BOTTOM LINE:

Relax.

STRATEGY #28

LEARN HOW TO FORGIVE

If you want to become a pro at six-sensory living and take full advantage of all the benefits it can offer you on the job, it's up to you to do everything in your personal power to show up to work alert, awake, and fully present in the moment. And nothing sabotages your ability to do so quite as thoroughly as being resentful of, or holding a grudge against, someone.

If you're mentally or emotionally consumed by the negative energy of an old injury, just know that more than 90 percent of your awareness will be distracted from the present moment because it's engaged in nursing your wounds from the past. Not only does carrying such resentments rob you of all ability to be fully present (a prerequisite to intuitive awareness), but it also causes you to shield yourself from further abuse by constructing defensive walls around yourself. Hunkered down and burdened by the past, the chances of your being accurately tuned in to the moment are virtually zero. So in order to create the success you desire today, you must immediately drop whatever baggage you're carrying from yesterday and beyond.

Now, having had my own feelings hurt a time or two, and understanding that being intuitive not only raises awareness but also sensitivity, I know how easy it can be to get upset or offended by someone at work (or anywhere in your life, for that matter). I also know that getting over it can be challenging, especially if you're feeling insecure. If you're really caught up in survival mode, releasing old grudges and moving on may even sound like professional suicide. Rest assured, I'm not suggesting that you go into denial over past injuries or condone anything destructive that's been done to you—I'm actually suggesting just the opposite.

The first and best way to forgive, forget, and move on when it comes to wounds from the past is to objectively examine what transpired from a spiritual perspective and get your ego out of the way. This means learning how not to take anything anyone has ever done to you personally, no matter how devious the behavior seems (and believe me, I know that when it comes to business, people can be devious). Despite all of the temptation for your ego to personalize other people's unsavory behavior, don't indulge in such self-destructive thinking . . . mostly because it isn't true.

You see, when people attack you, it's because they're caught up in their own negative issues and are just taking it out on the nearest punching bag—you. The more intuitive you become, the clearer this will be. People do what they do because of *their* goals, priorities, beliefs, and values; so, in reality, their assaults have nothing whatsoever to do with you, plain and simple.

The only way to truly forgive, forget, and move on is to take full responsibility for your own misjudgments and learn from them. And when you can't identify a misjudgment on your part, learn from the experience anyway.

Smart six-sensory people realize that on a soul level, everything happens for a reason, and the only thing to take from any event is what you can learn from it. When you shift your thinking in this way, the injury will immediately dissipate, your energy will lift, and you'll move out of negativity. Soon after, new doors will open that lead to more and better opportunities than you've ever had. Refuse the lesson, however, and the grudge will hang on, diminishing your awareness, draining your energy, and shutting doors to new possibilities.

For example, my client Martine, a fashion designer and owner of a small chain of clothing boutiques on the West Coast, was betrayed by one of her designers, an experience that made her extremely angry and bitter.

Martine told me that the one condition she'd given this guy was that, as a prospective partner, he sign a no-compete clause. It stated that should he ever start a business of his own, he wouldn't use anything he'd learned or acquired from Martine, including designs he'd created under her. Jumping at the chance for partnership and association with Martine's reputation, he readily agreed. In return, he was given an extremely generous salary and essentially the keys to two of my client's stores.

Two years later, in spite of his agreement, the designer left to open his own firm and virtually stole all of Martine's ideas. My client wasn't just livid, she was also hurt. She'd personally mentored this guy and given him her full support, not to mention a top-dollar salary and percentage of the business—so she couldn't understand why he'd abruptly taken all the money and the designs and run. Even as she called me for an appointment, Martine was plotting various strategies to get even. To her utter surprise, I said, "Forgive him and let it go."

"How can I forgive him after what he did to me?" Martine retorted, incredulous at my suggestion.

"Realize that he didn't do anything to you," I replied. "You told him he was a great designer, and he believed you. Rather than working for you, he wanted to become you."

"*Become* me?" Martine spat. "Achieving what I have will take a lot more than designs."

"Exactly," I said. "He'll see that soon enough, and he'll be back. So forgive him and move on."

"I don't want him back," Martine snarled. "He's an excellent designer and worker, but he's dishonest."

"Not in his mind," I answered. "He's just taking what you told him to heart and running with it, so forgive him. And watch—he'll be back. Besides," I pushed further, "is there any benefit to you in all of this? Wherever there's injury, there's also a gift, if you just look for it."

"Yeah, there's a gift," Martine smirked. "I overpaid him a lot and never should have offered him ownership so quickly. At least I got *that* back—and rightfully so."

"So be grateful for that much and let it go," I replied. "That way you won't be entangled in his energy, and you'll be freed up to make better decisions next time."

Martine was smart: She did forgive and forget and moved on. Just a few years later, the designer *was* back. His shop had failed, so he was now bankrupt and begging for his old job. Because Martine had forgiven him, she wasn't even angry anymore. If anything, she was amused. She'd prospered while he was away, partly due to recouping his original percentage of ownership. Desperate to work again, the designer asked for a third of his original salary and no ownership, and he even offered to work all the hours he needed to in order to get a second chance. Martine rehired him, and everyone benefited in the end.

Forgiveness is a very intelligent business policy, and by keeping your grudges few, not only will you keep your awareness sharp, but you'll also keep your eyes, ears, and heart open to whatever opportunities may present themselves. Also, particular industries tend to be very small fish bowls, and it's highly likely that you'll encounter the same people again and again throughout your career. By forgiving, you can always be comfortable—no matter whom you encounter at any time. Those who forgive keep moving along to greater and greater professional heights; those who don't just get victimized and lose out.

My client Carrie, together with another woman, created a business organizing other people's affairs, both in their homes and workplaces. They filed receipts, cleared closets, ran errands, helped people move their homes and businesses, and performed a thousand other mundane organizational tasks. Because they did it so well, their reputation grew and their business thrived. Clients began to trust them with more and more responsibility: Carrie and her partner were given passwords to computers, keys to homes, and even statements to bank accounts.

One day Carrie called me, nearly hysterical. Apparently her partner had confiscated a wealthy client's credit-card number and used it to charge thousands of dollars in purchases. She'd obviously gotten greedy over time and taken greater chances with the card, and she was finally caught. Needless to say, they were both fired. But worse, because they worked a tight-knit community, other clients got wind of the crime and also terminated their services, so they were essentially out of business overnight. Shocked, stunned, humiliated, and now unemployed, Carrie wanted to strangle her partner (or worse) and didn't know how to recover.

"Forgive her," I said, "and find the gift in this mess."

"How can I?!" she nearly screamed. "I can't even hold my head up in this town."

"Sure you can," I reassured her. "You aren't guilty of stealing, so *do* hold your head up high and forgive your partner for not being able to do the same. Stop kicking yourself for trusting her, learn from the experience, and move on. But first find the gift."

"The only gift in all of this," my client admitted, "was that I hated our business. It was my partner's idea to start it, and I just went along with it. The truth is, I'd long ago lost interest in the business and more or less let her take over, which is how this happened, I guess. At least now I don't have to clean up after people anymore."

"I'd consider that an excellent gift," I answered. "So take it for what it's worth and move on to something important to you. What would you like to do instead?"

"Believe it or not, I never minded sorting through people's stuff—it was putting things back together that was a problem for me," Carrie replied. "I used to say all the time, 'I should have been a private detective instead of an organizer. I'd be much better at that.'"

"So take the gift and do that. Become a detective," I suggested.

"Are you serious?" she asked with a chuckle.

"Yes, I am. Why not?"

My client laughed again, nervously at first, then with joy. "It couldn't be any more difficult than what we were doing," she mused. After a pause, she said, "I may just take you up on that."

Eighteen months later, Carrie sent me her wedding announcement. She actually had become a private detective and moved to Las Vegas, where she now worked in the casinos. She'd met the love of her life, a part-time card dealer and antique collector, on the job. And she was so delighted with how her life had turned around that she'd even asked her ex-partner to be her maid of honor. Apparently they'd resolved their differences along the way. I didn't ask how—it was obviously over, so why bring up the past?

12 SIMPLE STEPS TO FORGIVENESS

1. Don't take anything personally.
2. Don't attack yourself for mistakes.
3. Claim the gifts hidden in perceived injuries.
4. Take responsibility for the part you played in a particular situation.
5. See all events as opportunities for your soul to grow and mature.
6. Forgive yourself first.
7. Pray for help.
8. Develop a strong sense of humor.
9. Recommit to your goals and get back on track.
10. Count your blessings.
11. Stop rehashing past injuries—just don't talk about them anymore.
12. Focus on positive events.

Forgiving and moving on are not only good for business, they're also good for your health—especially when the person you need to forgive is *you.* Judging and blaming yourself for past mistakes and not moving on is one of the major causes of depression, stress, addiction, and anger. The longer you refuse to forgive and forget, the more pressure you put on your heart, your blood, and your arteries, all of which could spell the difference between living and dying in the long run. No grudge is worth holding on to to that degree.

Not forgiving yourself not only interrupts your business and health, but it also sours and destroys your relationships as well. It will drive the people around you crazy. So instead of lamenting yesterday's mistakes, get over it and do something better today. It's never too late.

A case in point is my brother-in-law Gene, a talented artist and sculptor who abandoned his true calling early in life and ended up taking over the family business instead. For a while it worked, but as he got older, he became more and more discontent. Eventually he deteriorated into a ball of anger and depression, all of which made it increasingly difficult for him to function day to day—and it made him unbearable to be around. While the business was easy enough for him to run, his heart just wasn't in it, and it showed. He felt it, his family felt it, and his clients felt it, causing his business to slide.

Finally, shortly after his 50th birthday, Gene became desperate to get over his depression and asked me for a reading, the first in all the years I'd known him. I told him what I've told other clients in the past: "You cannot be whatever you want and succeed. You can only be who you really are." I continued, "And you, Gene, are an artist. Your success depends on contributing your art to the world."

"I know you're right," he responded bitterly, "but if

I do what I want, I'm going to let my family down. No matter how I look at it, I see no way out, and it makes me really angry and resentful toward everyone, but mostly myself."

"Forgive yourself for all past decisions and move on from there," I advised. "The businesses you run aren't the problem, nor are the expectations of your family—avoiding your art is the problem, plain and simple. Your soul is heavy from not being yourself, and it's time to forgive this major mistake and get back to being you."

"At my age? In Dubuque? Isn't that irresponsible?" he asked, doubtful that his true calling could put food on the table.

"Even in Dubuque," I assured him. "Art is appreciated everywhere, so don't underestimate your crowd. Run the family business by day and do your art at night. Stop holding grudges, and turn that energy into creativity instead."

Gene took my suggestions to heart. Three months later, he donated his first professional piece, a beautiful sculpture he named "The Seeker," to the local art museum's annual fund-raiser. It was smashing success and commanded $1,900 for the auction . . . not bad for his first piece. Far more important, the president of a local bank approached my brother-in-law shortly after the evening ended and commissioned him to do two more pieces for the main branch, one for each entrance. And then, a lifelong friend who was very impressed with his work offered Gene a warehouse space to open a gallery to feature his work. Needless to say, his family couldn't have been more proud of him.

Gene was surprised at such a rapid and exciting turn of events in his life, but I wasn't. Such is the power of forgiving yourself and moving on, especially toward what's in your heart. You see, when you bear grudges, you totally shut down your heart, and with a closed heart you can't tune in to your vibes, as they *originate* in your heart.

When you hold grudges, you live in the past, rerunning past injuries over and over again in your mind like a bad movie. With your energy consumed in such a fashion, you have little awareness available in the present to notice and attend to the business at hand. When preoccupied with resentment, you listen less, hear less, and often care less about the people in front of you. And they feel it.

For example, just today I was out shopping with my daughter when we stopped in one of our favorite boutiques here in Chicago. Barely entering the door, we asked a salesperson if they carried a particular brand of jeans, only to be blasted with an arctic freeze of a response, followed by a wave of negative vibes toward the back of the store.

"What's her problem?" my daughter hissed underneath her breath as we headed toward the jeans.

"I have no idea," I answered, "but she sure has one."

Thirty seconds later, we overheard the woman ranting rather loudly about resenting her boss for asking her to work yet another weekend when she had other plans.

I had a good mind to call the store manager myself and ask him to give her the day off, as having her there was definitely bad for business; instead, my daughter and I decided to leave. As we walked toward the door, the salesperson interrupted her rant and asked us if we'd found everything we needed. "No," I answered, "we didn't. In fact, we feel uncomfortable in here for some reason and have lost the mood to shop."

I thought she got the point, but my daughter was sure she didn't. At any rate, I hope *you* do. If you're stuck in old negativity, guess what? Everyone around gets stuck in it, too . . . and they're not going to like it (or you) one bit. And don't think that you can hide your resentments from others—blame, bitterness, and judgment hold such toxic vibes that it's like hiding an elephant in the living room. Good luck.

Finally, forgiveness works both ways. If you're guilty of mistreating people or of being unethical in business, clean up your act. Your vibes are an indelible part of who you are, and your energy follows you wherever you go. If you cheat, manipulate, steal from, lie to, violate, or exploit others for your own personal gain, your negative energy will expose you. You may think that you're getting away with it, but success is far more than acquiring dollars—it's the ability to look at yourself in the mirror and like who's looking back.

Besides, we all have an inborn six-sensory radar, and sooner or later someone will use it to catch on to you. So think about the consequences of avoiding a life of decency and integrity. If you owe someone an apology, or you need to ask forgiveness or make amends to someone for your past mistakes, do so—that way you can call yourself a true success in every sense of the word.

The wisdom of forgiving, forgetting, and living a life of good vibes and clear energy in the moment cannot be overstated. Everything does happen for a reason, and there's always an opportunity hidden in every upset you face—or create. I'm not suggesting that you condone bad behavior, deny it, or hide it. All I'm saying is that you can stop playing the victim by no longer holding grudges or nursing wounds from the past, no matter who the culprit may be. Forgiveness puts the power for your future squarely back into your hands . . . and that's where it belongs. It's great for business and great for your life.

9 REASONS TO FORGIVE

1. It's good for your health.
2. It increases your longevity.
3. It increases your awareness and intuition.
4. It eases frown lines and costs less than Botox.
5. It improves your energy and attracts people to you.
6. It lifts your heart and creates positive vibes around you.
7. It makes life easier for you and everyone around you.
8. It increases your ability to be present, which translates into business dollars in the long run.
9. It sharpens your creativity.

So when you're thinking about the need to forgive and let go, consider the benefits to help motivate you. Start by looking for the gifts buried underneath all perceived injuries. With that gift in hand, forgiveness will come far more easily. Without claiming your gift, it's much easier to remain a victim . . . and why would you want that?

Your Turn

This week, write down a list of all the people you hold a grudge against in one column of your pocket notebook. Then, in another column, note all the gifts that came from these experiences. Mentally thank each person for the gift as you write. Better yet, say the following out loud: "I release myself from this experience and this person, and I take my power back in this moment."

Also, every time you find yourself dwelling on resentment, ask yourself if there's something you can do to recoup your sense of balance and peace over this issue. Remain grounded and neutral as you think this over. If there is, resolve to do it as soon as possible; if not, say, "I forgive, release, and let go of this now and forever."

If you know that you need to ask forgiveness of another, do so this week—you'll be glad you did. I've seen most people forgive quite easily once their feelings and point of view are acknowledged. You may very well find this out, too.

And finally, if resentment and anger are serious issues that you just can't get past, seek professional help. As long as you hold grudges and feel victimized, you're going to be stuck right where you are. This is no way to live, and certainly no way to succeed. There are many resources for resolving old wounds, so please take advantage of them. My favorite is an eight-day workshop called the Hoffman Quadrinity Process (**www.hoffmaninstitute.org**). This course has helped me move past some serious grudges in my life and has been incredibly healing—perhaps it may be useful to you, too. Otherwise, seek therapy or coaching to move yourself along. The sooner you do so, the better you'll feel—and the quicker you'll succeed in achieving all of your noble goals.

THE BOTTOM LINE:

Forgive them, for they know not what they do.

STRATEGY #29

GET SOME JOB INSURANCE

I'd just finished teaching an intuition workshop when I asked the audience if there were any questions. A dozen hands shot in the air, so I began calling on them one by one.

The first was an attractive, well-dressed woman in her 50s who asked, "How can I feel secure about my future? How will I know that I'm going to be okay?"

Intuitively seeing that she was very solidly employed and that her "security" wasn't an employment issue but an energetic one, I looked around the room and asked who else might share her question. Almost every hand in the room went up.

I reminded the group that a game the five-sensory mind likes to play is one of control—trying to be "sure of everything" before it feels safe. On the other hand, six-sensory awareness lets us know that this game of needing to be sure of things we can't control isn't a strategy for security, but rather one for permanent anxiety. To gain inner calm and security, especially on the job, is to give up all need to be sure and surrender your future well-being and safety to faith.

And true to form, when I suggested working with faith, the faces in the crowd became filled with incredulous stares. Faith to most five-sensories is no better than crossing your fingers and closing your eyes, hoping that the worst won't befall you. Yet understand that when I say *faith,* I'm not saying *fate.* I'm talking about confidence in the future based on what you do in the present—that is, if you show up to work faithfully every day and do your best, the doors of creative opportunity will keep opening.

In addition to faith, there's another tool you can take to work no matter what your job is or what the economy dictates, which will ensure your future and make you secure. That tool is the heartfelt intention to serve your fellow human beings with love in everything you do—a very different intention from "What's in it for me?"

Those who serve, whatever their function, leave an indelible imprint on others' souls and raise the vibration of others' hearts and energy in a profound way. Serving others with love elevates the vibrational frequency of any workplace to a very high level, creating peace, synchronicity, and flow. It not only makes your job go well, but it makes the experience and performance of everyone around you improve, too.

One of the most dynamic examples of this is Colleen Barrett, the president and chief operations officer of Southwest Airlines. With no college education, she began working as a secretary for a Texas lawyer with a philosophy she inherited from her mother: She never worried about what she could get out of a job, focusing instead on how she could best help others to get what they wanted. Throwing herself full force into the service of her many employers and fellow employees, Colleen eventually climbed up the corporate ladder and ended up running the nation's most profitable airline. Ask her how she did it, and she'll say: "With love, spelled *l-u-v,* and a deep commitment to serve my company, my employees, and my customers, in that order."

Colleen's recipe for job security, especially at a time when most other airlines are fighting for their lives, is worth considering. Southwest has been profitable for 30 years and has the lowest employee turnover of any airline. Asked why, the employees will say that it's because they feel loved and served by their company and strive very hard to do the same in return.

Although Southwest's philosophy sounds simple, the six-sensory wisdom of serving with love isn't widely practiced; thus, most people are left to flounder in fear and sink in their own insecurities. No one who works with genuine love and desire to serve ends up in an insecure corner, because this approach keeps vibrationally opening door after door for them.

SEVERAL YEARS AGO, A CLIENT NAMED Rhonda and her husband, Matt, opened a small travelers' coffee shop in my neighborhood that they called the Kopi Café. Having explored the world in earlier years and sharing a deep love of travel and travelers, Rhonda and Matt wanted to create a respite where fellow explorers could congregate, share stories, swap ideas about where to stay, and bring the world a little closer. The sole loving intention in opening this establishment was a desire to make voyagers' journeys sweeter.

Difficult at first because the neighborhood was in transition, Rhonda and Matt's adventure soon took off. People heard of the café and told others, and before long, the reputation spread. Not only did customers enjoy the international coffees, teas, cakes, and sweets at the café, they also found interested ears in Rhonda and Matt, who listened to their stories and helped them find support, comfort, and even a place to stay. The couple had time for everyone and encouraged their staff to do the same. Although it could be a little crazy at times, the atmosphere was always warm, welcoming, and festive. Even if you weren't a globe-trotter, going to Kopi gave you a taste of the world and offered instant adventure.

Rhonda showed up at my office pale with fear two years after the café had opened. Thanks in no small part to Kopi's success, the neighborhood had greatly improved, and she had just been informed that not one, but two big-chain coffeehouses were moving into the neighborhood in the next few months, and she was terrified that they'd put her out of business. She wondered how she could stop them.

Even though it looked ominous, I knew that Rhonda was in no danger whatsoever—after all, her customers got far more than a cup of coffee when they came to Kopi, and they knew it. Rhonda and Matt were immune to disaster if they simply continued to do what they loved *with* love and a desire to serve.

Reassured, but still nervous, Rhonda agreed that that was all she and Matt could do . . . so they did it even more. They opened a travelers' bulletin board; offered their fellow adventurers an opportunity to play music, tell stories, and entertain each other; and continued to serve and love their clientele.

Both chain coffee shops opened as predicted: The first closed within a year; the second survived, but catered to an entirely different crowd than Rhonda and Matt—who didn't lose a single customer. If anything, the contrast between their shop and the others only enhanced Kopi's reputation. And soon after, a neighborhood newspaper even featured

Kopi in an article touting its positive vibration.

I ran into Rhonda shortly afterward, and she laughingly said, "You were so right! The only way to be secure is to keep up the good vibes and have faith that they'll keep you going."

Another example of service and love as the best means of job security can be found in the story of my dear friends Gayle Seminara-Mandel and Howard Mandel, owners of Transitions Bookplace in Chicago. Starting out in a 400-square-foot shop on an obscure street almost 20 years ago, their devotion and service to customers not only provided the best bookstore specializing in consciousness-raising, but also a place to congregate as a community.

Now, having grown to a beautiful 3,000-square-foot establishment, Transitions is the leader in presenting consciousness-raising events in the Midwest. To know Gayle and Howard is to be loved by them, and walking into their store is as if you're walking into their living room. They embrace you. They know you by name. They ask about your family and remember what you tell them. Last week when I gave a talk about my latest work, they served cake and lemonade to the customers who were in line waiting for me to sign books. We all felt as though we were at a party at Gayle and Howard's home.

With chain and online stores eliminating independent bookshops one after the other, Transitions continues to be successful. People can buy the same items that this store sells for less elsewhere, but they choose not to—even when a major chain set up a store less than 500 feet away. It's a struggle, but Gayle and Howard are winning. People love Transitions because they feel so loved and served when they go there. And they'll keep going because the vibe is so good.

The bottom line is that you can't change the way the world turns, especially in work. The economic tides thrash about—rising, dropping, and turning every which way year after year. And it's apparent that no one is going to take care of you and protect you from the harsh vicissitudes of business. But you can take care of yourself if you refuse to get trapped by the fear and anxiety that terrorizes the five-sensory world. Instead, solidly align with the peace and tranquility of the six-sensory world by choosing to love through your work and serve your fellow human beings with your whole heart and soul.

The vibration of love and service is so powerful, healing, majestic, and rare that it keeps people coming back out of curiosity if nothing else—but then they'll stay because it feels so good. It's the best job insurance you can have.

Your Turn

This week, forget any insecurities and worries about the future, and choose instead to work with the intention to love and serve. See everyone you work with as a reflection of you, and realize that by doing so, you'll honor yourself. But don't confuse service with submission: To serve is to empower others; to submit is to disempower yourself.

In your pocket notebook, write down the names of all the people you choose to serve and how. Don't broadcast this to others as a way of gaining attention—keep it quiet, but do record these acts of service and their ensuing results for yourself. If at any time you feel small or resentful, forgive yourself and jot down at least ten similarities that you share with the people you're feeling negatively toward.

Admire what's in them that may need strengthening in you, and then admire in you what may need strengthening in them.

Work with love, and have fun serving those around you. Remember that the more you empower others, the more that vibration will return to empower you.

THE BOTTOM LINE:

Know that to serve is to rule.

A FINAL WORD

The best way to summarize the spirit of trusting your vibes at work can be found in this wonderful poem that was given to me by one of my most beloved colleagues—a person who I believe personifies six-sensory mastery in his work as an energetic healer—Dennis Kindle. I don't know who the author is, but I love it. I want to share it with you because I think it's so fantastic.

Master in the Art of Living,
I draw no distinction
between my work and my play,
my mind and my body,
my education and my recreation.
I simply pursue my vision of excellence
through whatever I am doing
and leave others to determine
whether I am working or playing.
To myself, I am always doing both.

I wish you all the best in creating and fulfilling your dreams and ambitions at work. Just remember: When in doubt, always and in all ways be true to yourself and trust your vibes. If you do, I promise that they'll work for you to direct you to the success you seek and more.

With love and good vibes,
Sonia

ACKNOWLEDGMENTS

I'd like to acknowledge David Smith for introducing me to Hay House and leading me into the best working relationship I've ever had in my professional life. Thank you, David—I'm so grateful.

To Reid Tracy, president of Hay House, thank you for being an inspirational leader, a fantastic personal mentor, and a great friend. Working with you has made my life a pure joy. You've taught me to trust and grow in ways I never dreamed possible, and I'm eternally grateful.

To Louise Hay, thank you for holding a standard and vision of beauty, integrity, generosity, and respect that's unprecedented and unparalleled in the workplace. I'm honored to be a member of the Hay House family.

To my teachers and mentors, Charlie Goodman and Dr. Trenton Tully, who taught me to trust my vibes in my own work and stay true to myself when the world didn't understand or accept me: Thank you for remaining with me in spirit even today.

To the hardworking team at Hay House—including Jill Kramer, Shannon Littrell, Christy

Salinas, Jacqui Clark, Angela Perez, and the entire marketing team for your behind-the-scenes support—your dedication and kind spirits have been wonderful gifts that bring me tremendous pleasure.

To my Translucent family—including my sister Cuky Harvey, Debra Grace, Karl Peschke, Dennis Kindle, Kimo Bradd, Michelle Robin, Crystal Jenkins, Kyle Peschke, and my daughters Sonia and Sabrina—thanks for creating the most incredible work experience ever. And to Lilly Pasleva, thank you for working so hard to help me all the time.

To Mark Welch, thank you for being a great ally and friend (and talent), and for sharing my passion for the work of spirit.

To my family—Patrick, Sonia, and Sabrina—thank you for allowing me to work as much as I do without resenting me.

To Nancy Levin, thank you for making my public presentations smooth and easy.

And a special thank you to my assistant, manager, and trusted ally Ryan Kaiser—your grounded and steady hand at the helm of this office has made every day a good day at work. Thank you, Ryan, you're the best. And to Ryan's mom, Ann: Thank you for turning my jumbled mess of papers into a readable manuscript.

I'd also like to thank Julia Cameron for being my sounding board; Linda Kahn and Bruce Clorfene for shaping and grounding this manuscript with their editorial skills; and all my clients for their stories, experiences, and willingness to trust in me.

I'm deeply grateful to you all.

ABOUT THE AUTHOR

Sonia Choquette is a world-renowned author, storyteller, vibrational healer, and six-sensory spiritual teacher in international demand for her guidance, wisdom, and capacity to heal the soul. She's the author of eight best-selling books, including *Diary of a Psychic* and *Trust Your Vibes,* and numerous audio programs and card decks. Sonia was educated at the University of Denver, the Sorbonne in Paris, and holds a Ph.D. in metaphysics from the American Institute of Holistic Theology. She resides with her family in Chicago.

Website: **www.soniachoquette.com**